Louis Adamic
A Checklist

Louis Adamic

A Checklist

By Henry A. Christian

Newark College of Arts and Sciences
Rutgers University

The Kent State University Press

The Serif Series

Bibliographies and Checklists, Number 20

William White, General Editor
Wayne State University

ISBN 0-87338-115-7
Library of Congress Catalog Card Number 76-634011
Manufactured in the United States of America
at the Press of The Oberlin Printing Company
Designed by Merald E. Wrolstad

First edition

For
Alexander P. Clark
and
France Adamič:
they made it possible for me
to be "of two worlds."

Contents

Preface

This volume undertakes to offer readers the first comprehensive bibliography of Louis Adamic's writing and selected materials about the man and his work. In preparing this book I have drawn on both the usual methods of investigation and three major sources. The first source—The Papers of Louis Adamic and Supplementary Materials in the Princeton University Library—represents more than three quarters of the Adamic material known to exist; and it has been my privilege to investigate, organize, contribute to, and catalogue that collection. The second source is the combined Yugoslav holdings of the Louis Adamic Collection in Narodna in Univerzitetna Knjižnica, at Ljubljana, and of the Louis Adamic Memorial Room in Praproče, the home in which Adamic was born, at Blato. The third source is the listing compiled in Zagreb by the staff of Jugoslovenski leksikografski zavod as a portion of the *Yugoslav National Bibliography: 1900–1945*, to be published sometime in the future; and the extensive, but not complete utilization of that listing here is to provide readers access to this hitherto unavailable information.

The text is divided into the seven sections detailed below, but a few general considerations apply equally to every section. It should be noted at the outset that I have paid more attention to the special tasks, as I construe them, of presenting Louis

Adamic than to the strictly formal rules of detailed bibliographical notation. On the other hand, because this volume may attract readers of widely different backgrounds, many entries are somewhat more complete than most methods of notation require. The order throughout the volume is chronological, by day and then month, with items of identical date being then ordered alphabetically. Discrepancies in the chronological order result from a publication's using material from another publication whose availability usually preceded its published date of issue, or from the inclusion of material from the Zagreb source which I could not myself verify. Such entries from the Zagreb source may be identified by the presence of an issue number rather than a day or month date, and the absence of such dates often caused these entries to be listed alphabetically at the end of the year in which that item was published. Items so marked but dated more recently than 1945, however, have been taken from *Slovenska Bibliografija* (Ljubljana), Vols. I–XIV, or from *Bibliografija Jugoslavije* (Beograd), and may also lack page notations. But it should be made clear that in many instances the Zagreb source provided sufficient information for me to place such entries in the proper chronological order and that only one of those verified proved inaccurate, leading me to believe in the general reliability of all the Zagreb material. Those entries missing information are items which I could not see in total but whose authenticity is verified by their presence in Adamic's scrapbooks, clipping files, and the like, at Princeton and Ljubljana.

In many instances during the early part of his career Adamic was not acknowledged by editors and publishers who accepted his translations from other languages, and again authenticity for such items has been established by investigation of the materials at Princeton and Ljubljana. Such was the procedure too for anonymous and pseudonymous items. Save for letters and notes, Adamic wrote very little in any language but English; readers should assume, therefore, that unless otherwise noted all titles not in English in Sections I–VI are translations of Adamic's work, the translator's name or other identification being given when known. It should also be noted that many Yugoslav and domestic Slavic language publications sometimes vary the language or alphabet, or both, which they employ within a single article or issue. Thus, an entry marked "Cyr." indicates that the text is printed in Cyrillic, despite the fact that the title is given here in the Latin alphabet. Furthermore, the wide range of Adamic's work led to an equal diversity in the periodicals which printed material by or about him; and specialists in many different fields will have rather varying degrees of familiarity with many of the publications listed here. It was just a year ago, for example, that a nationwide effort was begun to identify and create centralized depositories for America's domestic foreign language press. I have thus provided the place of publication for a number, but hardly all, of those periodicals cited here. I have also otherwise annotated certain entries when such additional information seemed useful.

The specific sections of the bibliography and details pertaining to each are as follows:

I. Periodicals. This section includes Adamic's translations, stories, articles, book reviews, letters to editors, broadsides, and appeals published in periodicals. Many of these items were reprinted, in whole or in part, both during and after Adamic's lifetime. In order to illustrate further the size and variety of Adamic's readership, changes in titles and other places and dates of publication for such reprinted items are given below the main entry. An item which is doubly indented and marked with an asterisk represents a reprinting from the source immediately above it rather than from the source stated in the main entry.

Adamic regularly included in his books work previously published in periodicals, but he sometimes revised such pieces significantly. When a periodical publication was the result of his sending off a portion of a work-in-progress or his including already published material as part of a new book, the item appears without further notation as a main entry. But if the periodical publication was noted as a reprint from a book, the source of that item is given at the end of the entry. Initial entries which represent translations of Adamic's work have his original title in brackets immediately after the foreign title. However, translations which are reprintings, and therefore indented, bear only the foreign title, unless that title tends to differ in meaning from Adamic's original. It is hoped that these textual methods will make it possible for a reader to have before him the history of a single item through perhaps several decades. The story "A Bohunk Woman," for example, illustrates how in some instances an original periodical publication underwent a striking series of reprintings (see nos. 91–91f). Appearing first in the *American Mercury* in 1930, "A Bohunk Woman" was included by Adamic in *Laughing in the Jungle*. The second periodical appearance of the story occurred in the fledgling English language *South Slav Herald* (Belgrade and London) on the occasion of Adamic's Guggenheim visit to Yugoslavia, and the *Herald* editor noted the item as a reprinting from *Laughing in the Jungle*. The story was thereafter translated into Slovenian and Serbo-Croatian and appeared in three different Yugoslav publications, then reprinted again in English in the American newspaper *Slovak Democrat*, and finally translated into Italian and reprinted.

Adamic was the founder and only editor of *In Re: Two-Way Passage* (Vol. I, no. 1—Vol. II, no. 9; January, 1942—August–September, 1943), which was subsequently titled *War and Post-War* (Vol. II, no. 10—Vol. III, no. 12; October, 1943—

November–December, 1944), *Today & Tomorrow* (Vol. I, no. 1; January, 1945), and finally *T & T: Trends and Tides* (Vol. I, no. 2—Vol. VI, no. 2; March–April, 1945—Mid-Spring, 1950). He was the first editor of *Common Ground* (Vol. I, no. 1—Vol. II, no. 2; Autumn, 1940—Winter, 1942), and he then served on the Advisory Editorial Board of *Common Ground* (Vol. II, no. 3—Vol. IV, no. 3; Spring, 1942—Spring, 1944). He was also the first editor of *The Bulletin of the United Committee of South-Slavic Americans* (Vol. I, no. 1—Vol. II, no. 5; September 7, 1943—May 10, 1944). Although Adamic's major contributions to these three periodicals are here listed in full, his minor editorial notes have been omitted. For these and an understanding of Adamic's general involvement in the functions of these publications, it is suggested the reader consult the journals directly.

II. Pamphlets and Books. This section also includes those pamphlets and books edited by Adamic, those listing him with others as authors, and those wholly created by the reprinting of his work. Significant textual changes following first editions and editions and translations by different publishers are indented below the main entries, with full titles repeated.

III. Forewords and Other Minor Contributions to Pamphlets and Books.

IV. Portions of Books Reprinted in Pamphlets and Books by Others. The reprintings listed here had no previous American periodical publication and thus differ from such items in section I.

V. Special Materials in the Princeton University Library. This section lists items which contain the words or ideas of Adamic presented in a form which makes such items generally unavailable outside the collection at Princeton. Materials such as MSS, typed revisions, corrected galley proofs, correspondence, and personal notes have, to the best of my knowledge, not been included.

VI. Special Materials in Narodna in Univerzitetna Knjižnica, Ljubljana, Yugoslavia. The limitations for the Princeton items of section V apply also to Ljubljana items.

VII. A Selected List of Biographical and Critical Materials about Louis Adamic. This section presents a significant sample of printed materials about Adamic. Many of the entries amplify items in the foregoing sections. Indeed, both by choice and by accident of availability, I have included in several instances concentrations of material concerning a particular subject or period of time from one or more publications. Furthermore, the entries in this section come fittingly from the three major areas of Adamic's literary life—slightly less than half from American publications, almost a quarter from domestic foreign language publications printing as well at times in English, and the remainder from foreign publications. In no sense, however, should the reader consider the listings of this section anything more than a sample. It must be remembered that Adamic's career spanned the years when the literary columns of even daily newspapers were filled with publishing gossip and summaries of articles in the leading periodicals, and Adamic's files and scrapbooks at Princeton and Ljubljana attest to the fact that he received his fair share of such notices, to say nothing of the announcements and summaries of his lectures on the woman's or society pages of city and town newspapers throughout the country. In fact, had I completed the partial entries for American newspapers alone still remaining in the material at Princeton and Ljubljana, this section could easily be doubled. Similarly, although some reviews of Adamic's books are included here, no concerted effort has been made to record such items. Adamic's books were often reviewed abroad and thoroughly reviewed in the literary journals and newspapers of most major cities in America, and reports of his clipping services indicate that syndication of such reviews in the newspapers of lesser cities was common. The reader seeking reviews is thus directed to those book sections and review digests which he finds most readily available. In this section I have again drawn on the Zagreb listings; but I have not here provided translations of foreign titles, believing that those readers whose interest in this material exceeds the general idea of quantity will have the necessary language skills. An asterisk has again been employed in this section when an item was specifically noted to have been reprinted from a source other than the main entry.

Throughout the volume, the absence of certain accents required for the letters *C*, *S*, *Z*, *c*, *r*, and *y* is due to the unavailability of type.

Acknowledgements

Since this work is the outgrowth of an Adamic biography-in-progress, in some measure I owe a debt to the several hundred people who have aided me in that larger undertaking. For specific contributions to this volume, however, I should like to thank, and release from any fault herein, the following institutions, organizations, and individuals: the New York Academy of Medicine; the Carnegie Corporation; the Guggenheim Foundation; the New York Public Library; the staff of the Center for Research Libraries in Chicago; Mary S. Pratt, History Department, and Lois M. Jones, Literature Department, Los Angeles Public Library; Horace F. Hilb, Manuscript Division, the Library of Congress; Mrs. Hanny Cohrsen and Read Lewis, Director Emeritus, of the American Council for Nationalities Service; M. Sokitch, Editor of *American Srbobran*; Joseph A. Colkar of the Slovene National Benefit Society; Louis Beniger, Editor of *Prosveta*; Hazel Johnson, Palmer Library, Connecticut College; Tay Hohoff of J. B. Lippincott Company; Helen Lane, Beulah W. Hagen, and Cass Canfield of Harper and Row; Mark Movrich of the Sun Newspapers, Wisconsin and Minnesota. And in Yugoslavia, Edvard Kardelj; Mira Mihelič; Josip Vidmar; Janko Tompa; Dr. Boris Kuhar, Director of Slovenski Etnografski Muzej; Radojka Vrančič and Dr. Jaro Dolar, Director of Narodna in Univerzitetna Knjižnica; Branko Hanž and Milutin Ivanušic of Nacionalna i sveučiliňa biblioteka, Zagreb; and most especially Dr. Oto Oppitz and the staff of Jugoslovenski leksikografski zavod and Louis Adamic's nephew, Dr. Tine Kurent of the University of Ljubljana. And also, Jack Conroy; Mrs. Margaret Vanka; Carey McWilliams; the late Frankie Adams (Mrs. Alexander Gumberg); Dr. and Mrs. Harold Sanders; Timothy Seldes and Bucklin Moon; Professor Edward S. Allen of Iowa State University; Mr. and Mrs. Ben Zukor; and M. Margaret Anderson.

I am grateful as well to the Rutgers University Research Council which supported my work and travel in the United States and Yugoslavia by a Council Grant, a Summer Fellowship, and a Faculty Fellowship; and to Janko N. Rogelj of the Louis Adamic Memorial Foundation, without whom there would be no detailed Adamic studies in the United States.

Different but equally sincere thanks go also to the following: Professor Matthew Bruccoli of the University of South Carolina, for remembering; C. Howard Allen of the Kent State University Press, for patience and understanding; Vera Golob, for translations which made much of this volume possible; Margaret Bandrowski, for research and proofreading which made all of my Adamic work possible; my colleague George Groman, for constant belief in the Adamic project; my friend William K. Bottorff of the University of Toledo, for constant belief in me; Professor George Monteiro of Brown University, for kindness and example; and Professor Hyatt H. Waggoner of Brown University, for past and future lessons and criticism. While I could not but learn from them, the following at the Princeton University Library always kindly made me believe I was their equal: Mina R. Bryan, Howard C. Rice, Earl E. Coleman, Julie Hudson, and Wanda Randall. But the final, greatest debt is to those to whom this volume is dedicated.

HENRY A. CHRISTIAN

Princeton, New Jersey

Introduction

In 1937 Louis Adamic found that he had achieved a fame sufficient to generate a constant interest in the pronunciation of his surname, and he prepared a mimeographed reply to those who sought such information by mail. For Adamic readers, old and new, who are hesitant about his name, the introduction to this checklist begins with two quotations.[1] The first is from Adamic's mimeograph:

> To inquiries about the "correct" pronunciation of my surname I take—with apologies—this means of replying:
>
> In my native Slovenia, my family name is ADAMIC, with a little hook over the *c*, which makes it *ch* as in "rich." The Slovenian pronunciation is *Ah-dah-mich*, both *a*'s being rather full and long, with the accent on the middle syllable.
>
> In the U.S. I drop the hook over the *c*, because what it does to the pronunciation of *c* is generally unknown here. This makes the name either *A-dam'ic*, as the English word "Adamic," meaning "pertaining to Adam" is pronounced according to Webster, or *Ad'amic*, the *c* being the equivalent of *k* and the accent falling on the first syllable.
>
> Personally, I favor the latter, but have no deep objection to other pronunciations—not even *Ah-dahm'eesh*, which is what usually happens when non-Slavic persons in this country who have heard of the old-country pronunciation make a try at it.[2]

[1] Portions of this introduction appeared in "Ten Letters to Louis Adamic" in *The Princeton University Library Chronicle* and are here reprinted with permission of the *Chronicle*.

[2] Although I have not footnoted quotations from Adamic, all quotations from

The second quotation is a notice the compiler of this volume kept tacked above his desk for several years and used in lieu of a mimeograph to visitors whose questions concerned Adamic's Anglicized Christian name:

> His name was spelled *Louis* and always pronounced as if he were a king of France.[3]

But however necessary this information may be for some, such material might still have been reduced here to a footnote were it not for the fact that Adamic's consideration of his name exemplifies a process he underwent for many different subject matters throughout his life. One easily discerns the 1937 mimeograph as an important step in the author's progress from the young man who begins to publish in the *American Mercury* in the 1920s because he knows he is still the immigrant Alojzij Adamič to the internationally known Louis Adamic who writes *What's Your Name?* in the 1940s because he will not forget that he, with so many others, was foreign born. For Adamic, then, what began as an inescapable private concern eventually grew to a general consideration of the lives of millions. And that is equally true for most of the other situations in which he found himself or into which he thrust his energies. His need to investigate rather than merely make a place for himself—his desire to become a writer rather than merely literate—led him to delve into nearly every aspect of American life; and his gigantic enthusiasms often probed for responses that lay deep in the hearts of those who came to know his work. Today the writing detailed in the following pages may be classified under many labels: immigration and acculturation, to be sure, but

unpublished Adamic material are here published with the exclusive permission granted me by the Adamic family in Yugoslavia.

[3] In *What's Your Name?* Adamic remarked: "Some people pronounce the *s*; others leave it silent. Either way is all right with me." I have encountered no one who knew Adamic well, however, who pronounced the *s*.

also the 1920s, the depression, labor and unions, progressive and liberal thought, civil rights, foreign policy, Communists, and "Communists"—these last two being distinct terms Adamic often employed. Indeed, Adamic's investigations were so naturally a function both of his personality and talents and of his life as an immigrant and naturalized citizen that—if Oscar Handlin's discovery that immigrants are American history is valid—Adamic to a great degree *is* American history for his time.

Louis Adamic was born on March 23, 1898, in the village of Blato, in Slovenia, which was then a province of Austria-Hungary but in 1918 become the north-west portion of Yugoslavia. Although the eldest son and by peasant tradition supposed eventually to inherit his father's land, Adamic proved an able scholar during his first four years of instruction at the district school in Grosuplje and was sent on to Ljubljana to pursue studies which would prepare him to enter the Roman Catholic seminary—a plan not at all uncommon for Slovenian youths who displayed intellectual promise. But his doubts about a clerical life and his high-spirited though nonetheless punishable participation in the student activities of the Yugoslav National Movement terminated his studies five years later. He was never to have formal education again. Late in December of 1913 he passed through Ellis Island and began residence with relatives in New York.

For two years Adamic was employed in the mail room and then the editorial office of the Slovenian language newspaper *Glas naroda*, but in 1916 he left the paper and spent a few months on his own as a laborer. That December he enlisted in the army and served in Panama, Louisiana—where he became a naturalized citizen—and Hawaii. He remained in the army until January of 1923. Much of his postwar duty was at Fort McArthur, San Pedro, California; and he settled in the harbor town after his discharge.

Adamic published original material in *Pearson's Magazine* while he was still in the army; but for the first few years in San Pedro he faced his military duty by day and struggled with English grammar in the evening, and much of his work consisted of translations from Slavic authors. When in 1925 he became a clerk in the municipal port pilots' office, however, he had a job which allowed him more time to write. He became a regular contributor to the several Haldeman-Julius publications and continued to place his translations in *Our World*, *The Living Age*, the Chicago Slovenian daily *Prosveta*, and other similar periodicals. One Slavic author whom he often translated was Ivan Cankar. In 1926, at the beginning of a lifelong acquaintanceship, Upton Sinclair brought Adamic to the attention of the newly established Vanguard Press. Within a few months that house published *Yerney's Justice*, Adamic's rendering of Cankar's novelette *Hlapec Jernej in njegova pravica.*

The cover of each *Haldeman-Julius Monthly* carried a cartoon showing a man flicking ink from the nib of a straight pen into the face of an obese character labeled "Bunk"; and between 1925 and 1928, when his work was often the feature article in the *Monthly*, Adamic had little difficulty finding suitable subjects amid the social aberrations of life in Los Angeles. He called the city "The Enormous Village," and he specialized in personalities who, he felt, trafficked in the spiritual and intellectual weaknesses of the public. Yet Haldeman-Julius was not for Adamic the main debunker, nor were the frauds of Los Angeles his sole interest. He was more devoted to H. L. Mencken and aspired to the better literary material of the *American Mercury*. Thus he was delighted when in 1927 Mencken accepted his article "The Yugoslav Speech in America" and several more articles and stories in the next months. By 1930 Adamic had placed eight items in the *Mercury*, and during the next decade he and Mencken often found one another's projects of interest.

The subject matters of Adamic's contributions to the *American Mercury*—the army, his fellow immigrants, his acquaintances, and himself—indicate in part the broad base of old experience and new adventures he was attempting to capture, combine, and make live during these years. In San Pedro alone he had abundant stimulation for his restless and probing imagination. At the pilot station or among the Croatians at the cannery or on the piers of Fish Harbor he learned the port's public and private life, from buncombe to bootlegging, from pathos to piety. He bought an automobile and drove along the coast or into the desert, looking, listening, and always coming home with information, and more questions. He was a constant collector and interrogator at several Los Angeles book shops. His acquaintances were many and varied. George Sterling recommended him to a young lawyer and writer, Carey McWilliams, who in turn interviewed him, included him in his "Southern California Begins to Write" series for *Saturday Night*, and then took him along on several interviews of other authors. One such visit in 1928 was to Una and Robinson Jeffers at Tor House, from which Adamic, with Una Jeffers' willing aid, produced *Robinson Jeffers: A Portrait*. Adamic also became interested in the 1910 bombing of the Los Angeles *Times* building; and by the summer of 1929 he was at work on a book about the incident and had decided to move to New York to be closer, he rationalized, to potential publishers. But his real reason was to be near a Hunter College student, a Jewess named Stella Sanders, whom he had met in Los Angeles and was to marry two years later.

Those who met Adamic once he arrived in New York saw a dark, tall, muscular, rather handsome, young man. His speech contained just the trace of an accent; and because he stammered at times, he had a tendency to be shy, yet when amused could also erupt suddenly with a broad smile and booming laughter. Through the autumn of 1929, the promise of an advance from Alfred A. Knopf kept him steadily at work on the *Times* book. But the poor quality of the manuscript and the tensions of a nation shaken by the ruin in Wall Street combined to cause Knopf to refuse what Adamic turned in. His finances and hopes dropped steadily until July of 1930 when, with the help of his agent Maxim Lieber and the encouragement of Burton Rascoe, he signed with the Viking Press a contract for what was essentially a different book. During the next months he worked tirelessly in the New York Public Library on what finally became *Dynamite*, his study of labor violence in America.

Dynamite was more successful than even Adamic had hoped; and despite the fact that in March of 1931 the Guggenheim Foundation turned down his application for a fellowship, the year proved better for him than for many others. He widened his acquaintance with literary New York, did some book reviewing, and published a number of notable articles, the most memorable of which is "New England's Tragic Towns" in *Harper's Magazine*. In the autumn he submitted a second Guggenheim application, married Stella Sanders, and then went off to spend several weeks as a guest at Yaddo, the writers' colony in Saratoga Springs, New York, where he worked on *Laughing in the Jungle*. By January of 1932 the galleys of that book and an improved list of sponsors, including now H. L. Menckin, Sinclair Lewis, Mary Austin, the anthologist E. J. O'Brien, and Carl Sandburg, had won him a Guggenheim Fellowship for fiction.

Adamic and his wife sailed for Europe intending to visit several countries, including Russia, but found it impossible to progress beyond their initial stop in Yugoslavia. Adamic had, after all, no mature knowledge of his parents, his nine younger brothers and sisters, or his native land. Besides, he was hailed as both a returning son and an author of some reputation. He did know that occasionally he was reviewed and translated "at home," but he was unprepared for the attention paid to him. Even had his emotions been less fully captured by the experience, it would have been impossible for an observer-writer of Adamic's temperament to ignore the opportunities of the situation. He began at once to write about various aspects of his homecoming, and those pieces which he sent to America were well received. And he found most of his Yugoslav audience equally congenial. *Dynamite* and *Laughing in the Jungle* were published in translation in Zagreb. A Ljubljana house collected a number of his translated articles into a little volume titled *Kriza v Ameriki.* The Slovenian *Ljubljanski Zvon* printed both his old and new work, and he oversaw an "American issue" of the journal for which he collected an interesting range of material by other authors. Once he decided to remain in Yugoslavia for his Fellowship year, he set out to see the country and, as usual, question and record all he encountered. By December he wrote his publisher that he had nearly finished the novel proposed to the Guggenheim board, although having said so he put the manuscript aside in favor of the more immediate material of his travels.

Adamic had hardly begun his tour, however, before he learned that his visit had left Ljubljana in turmoil. He had been accepted by all the Slovenian *literati* from the very start, but he had gravitated somewhat to those who were more liberal in both social and political matters. His dealings with the objective *Ljubljanski Zvon* had upset those writers who supported the conservative *Dom in svet*, the organ of the Clerical Party and the first Slovenian journal to review his work. Matters became worse when the respected poet Oton Zupančič published "Adamič in slovenstvo" in the *Zvon*. Zupančič's view of what, for want of a better term, must be called Slovenianism generated numerous differing interpretations, and Adamic found himself and his work at the center of a literary war over the definition of Slovenian culture. Several years later when Adamic discussed the matter in *My America*, he noted that to a population of more than one hundred million the episode probably appeared ridiculous. Nevertheless, at the time those of his readers who knew the cultural pride of small nations could fully understand the event; and today it is clear Adamic was a part of a major Slovenian conflict which was not so much resolved as engulfed by subsequent history.

Adamic returned to America in the spring of 1933 and began to revise his Yugoslav material into the book *The Native's Return*. The work was the Book-of-the-Month Club selection for February of 1934 and an instant success. Before long Adamic found himself a celebrity and harder at work than ever. He was placed on the Executive Board of the Foreign Language Information Service; it was a fortunate union of a man who never lost interest in every aspect of immigration and an organization whose contacts with government agencies, the foreign language press, and the individual immigrant were both extensive and practical. He was one of seven people honored at a luncheon sponsored by The League for Political Education. He was called to Washington to discuss the possibility of resettling ethnically homogenious, depression ridden urban populations in unoccupied farm land. He issued a revised edition of *Dynamite*. He set out on a lecture tour to publicize his book and to survey America. He had until then written about those aspects of American life he knew by necessity. Now he was more free to exercise his curiosity, to visit new places, in hope of discovering all of the nation. In increasing numbers he encountered nationality groups, officials of labor and government and educational organizations, and citizens in general of varying backgrounds and employment. To some audiences he was a best-selling author, to others he was a dynamic personality, to still others he was a brother immigrant who had made good. And when on occasion his stammer made him halt abruptly while he fought his uncooperative jaw for his next word, he was to nearly everyone a truly dedicated man. In the cities and towns he visited, his remarks began to be noted in both the local newspapers and the domestic foreign language press serving the area.

It took Adamic only a short time to realize that the complexity of America, within which he had toiled and about which he had written for survival, was no less remarkable now that he had emerged and consciously sought to define it. Sections of *The Native's Return* and some of his articles irritated one or another American Yugoslav group. American Serbs condemned his judgment of King Alexander's dictatorship and the prediction of that monarch's assassination. Segments of the immigrant Catholic Church saw Communism in his statement that the national survival of Yugoslavia lay in a Balkan federation of nations attached to Russia "in some mutually satisfactory way." The state of the literary world at the time proved no less adventuresome. In 1933 the *New Masses* published "What It Means to Be a Communist in Yugoslavia," Adamic's translation of a manuscript "by a young Communist" who had been tortured under the Alexander regime. Then in 1934 Adamic's anti-fascist commitment was judged insufficient, and the magazine attacked him for not including the document in *The Native's Return*. When in "What the Proletariat Reads" he suggested the proletariat did not read at all, he was declared an enemy of the worker by the Marxist critics and defended by the editor of *The Anvil* and author of *The Disinherited*, Jack Conroy. Had he the time, Adamic might well have thought he was back in Ljubljana. But he met these and other incidents head on. Even when he disagreed, he understood the sensitivity of the immigrant and his family on matters of heritage and adjustment. He knew that to be "Americanized" was to suffer the loss of valuable traditions; he knew too that to remain totally "foreign" meant isolation. First and foremost, however, he was learning that to maintain a balance between the two courses was a delicate, perpetually arguable and perhaps impossible matter involving everyone, especially in a world of fragmented and shifting alignments. His first lecture tour had given him a taste of this investigation, and he intended in future trips to seek what he came to call the "unity in diversity" of America. That he was far from conservative was obvious, but that he would conform to no program was equally clear.

If Adamic's political position in 1934 or at any time during the decade can be described at all, he somewhat fits the second of three classifications of liberalism formulated by F. A. Warren—"one who was more impressed by the Russian 'experiment' than by Communist doctrines; who was sympathetic, though not entirely uncritical, toward the Soviet Union, without necessarily accepting the Communist line on other topics."[4] Years before he had told Upton Sinclair that he could no longer believe in causes; and after 1930 he argued that no American revolution was just around the corner, that indeed, revolution would not be the process by which America would change. He saw his adopted country as a confusing complex with an infinite potential, and he was going to try to explain and guide her as best he could. His general distrust of all organizations and his desire for the individual freedom and development of all men had early put him at odds with American Marxists and led him more than once to retort to

[4] *Liberals and Communism: The "Red Decade" Revisited* (Bloomington, 1966), p. 5. Within the limitations Warren set himself, he is correct in differing with me by placing Adamic in his third classification—"anti-Communist" liberals.

those who would settle for nothing short of "a side" that he was at heart an anarchist. "Basically, I suppose," he wrote in *My America* a few years later, "I am a student who is his own teacher, a finder-out, one who is trying to get at the truth about things and making an effort to understand them. . . . I want to be, to do something, to spend myself for something." Of course, in his career thus far he had been no less subjective than the next man; and it was apparent to him that if America were to achieve the potential of "unity in diversity," it *would* be through organization and individual leadership. In fact, the most significant personal dilemma in Adamic's career, especially after 1940, was that his activities offered him power which he would not refuse but in which he did not fully trust. By the close of 1934, then, Adamic had more than begun the work by which, to "foreigners" and native Americans alike, he would finally become, for good or evil, both a symbol and a voice of the diversity from which the nation was continually being made whole. Yet when he resumed *Grandsons*, the novel begun in Yugoslavia, both a national and a somewhat personal condition was indicated when he had his narrator describe Americans as "shadows flitting over the face of this beautiful continent."

During 1935 Adamic published *Grandsons* and produced a number of articles from his experiences and observations in various parts of the country. He absorbed all he encountered and soon decided to write the book *My America*, although at the time he said he preferred to title it as he had, tongue-in-cheek, one of his current lectures—"A Country Full of Nice People." He tried to interest the Federal Emergency Relief Administration in an encyclopedia of the population of the United States. Now and again he became especially excited by a place or an idea he considered unique and would want to spread the news wholesale. Typical of these "infectious enthusiasms," as a friend of his called such episodes, was Black Mountain College.[5] Arriving for a brief inspection of the institution, Adamic stayed on in North Carolina for several weeks and then produced a lengthy manuscript. When *Harper's Magazine* accepted the contribution on condition that it be cut to usual article size, Adamic raged that he could have, indeed should have, written a book about the College. He also now turned his attention to a volume of Slavic material in translation, a collection of his own work and that of others. Unable to convince a publisher of the value of such a book, he let the idea drop under the pressure of more urgent tasks. For the remainder of his life, however, he would occasionally attempt the volume; and it was a great disappointment to him that he was never able to offer the material to an English-speaking audience.

By now Adamic had set himself a pace which only a man of his particular background, determination, and enthusiasm could maintain. He published *Cradle of Life*—a novel based in part on the life of his friend, the Croatian painter Maxo Vanka. What was to be nothing but a much needed vacation in Guatemala in the winter of 1936 led to *The House in Antigua.* That too, he wrote his editor, was a part of America. Furthermore, there were articles to be done on John L. Lewis, Harry Bridges, strikes, immigration, and much more. In 1938 he finally published *My America,* adding still another personal portrait of the nation to an already large number of volumes which had been initiated by the agonies of the decade—a book, as Alfred Kazin noted, of "social 'reportage' " typical of those "whose authors were always seeking to catch reality on the run."[6]

For Adamic, *My America* represented only a partial culmination of the determined investigation of the United States

[5] I am indebted to that friend, the late Frankie Adams (Mrs. Alexander Gumberg), for the term.

[6] *On Native Grounds* (New York, 1942), p. 494.

which began in 1934. As candid and characteristic of both the author and the times as was the book, it could be but a stop on what Adamic, citing Arthur E. Morgan, referred to as "the Long Road . . . the American way." Two years earlier he had decided the subjects he was attempting to treat would require several volumes—a series, in fact, for which he selected as a title the Whitman phrase "a nation of nations."

Early in 1937 he had purchased Mountain View Farm near Milford, New Jersey, and with the award of a Rockefeller Foundation grant-in-aid had finally been able to begin to implement years of experience and planning. With hardly a break in order to prepare *My America* for publication, he expanded the processes which eventually transformed his home and outbuildings into an extensive depository of the personal reminiscences, problems, and hopes of immigrants and their children. "This is how you look in Finnish," the Director of the Foreign Language Information Service once wrote at the top of a page torn from the daily newspaper *Raivaaja*; and even today one can only guess at the number of unrecorded translations or notices of Adamic's work which may have appeared in the domestic foreign language press. Then in 1938, in order to supplement his research trips, he flooded both foreign and English language publications of all kinds with requests for information about immigrants and second and third generation Americans. He combed directories and registries in search of names and addresses to which he could send specialized questionnaires—"To Polish Americans," "To Jewish Americans," "To a Selected List of People Known To Be Interested. . . ." He developed a broadside titled "Plymouth Rock and Ellis Island" and distributed it widely to organizations, institutions, and individuals in order to obtain pertinent material. In 1939 he sent out a lengthy mimeographed document titled "Let's Become Americanized—ALL OF US," with half of each page left blank for notes by readers. A year later he saw into print *From Many Lands*. This volume won the John Anisfield Award as "the most significant book of 1940 on race relations in the contemporary world."

Adamic followed his Rockefeller grant with support from the Carnegie Corporation. *From Many Lands* was the first of the four works in his Nation of Nations Series which he would accomplish, long after the money ceased, in fulfillment of what he considered a promise to the Corporation. Furthermore, the book *was* finally indicative of the full range of involvement he had so long striven to capture and explain. His characters were dramatized from his acquaintances and investigations, and in their separate episodes they touched nearly all of the "diversity" he had insisted should be understood in order to accomplish America's complete "unity." They were the "traditional" immigrants, to be sure; but they also included a wealthy, second generation, American Jew professionally famous in his own right, a Mexican resisting assimilation as a "U. S. American," and a rootless California-born Japanese youth—the children and grandchildren of immigrants and the less integrated, less considered, and more restricted immigrants. The people behind the labels here emerged more clearly than ever, and a host of collateral biases that lay hidden within racial considerations were also exposed to the reader. In addition, although in his final remarks Adamic explained that groups he had neglected would be included in future volumes, he did bring full circle the problem of America's incomplete society and potential by at least mentioning the American Indian and by reprinting his mailing titled "Special Questionnaire on the Negro." "Can you," he asked of both white and Negro correspondents, "isolate the so-called Negro Problem from the entire racial-cultural problem in America? Isn't it part of the same vast complexity which involves us all and is a matter of general prejudice and intolerance, of ignorance and fear?"

By 1940 the war in Europe gave added meaning to the past achievements and the proposed tasks of the Foreign Language Information Service. The organization changed its name to Common Council for American Unity and began to publish the quarterly *Common Ground*, a journal devoted to the creation of unity and mutual understanding among peoples of diverse backgrounds in America. Founded and first edited by Adamic, *Common Ground* carried forward the goals he promulgated in *From Many Lands* and especially emphasized the value of Americans of foreign background in a country which more and more was choosing sides by nationality trait. Adamic deplored the increase of bias and feared that, whether or not America entered the war, widespread hatred would reach its most dangerous level once Europe was at peace again.

Before the March, 1941, two-day alliance between Yugoslavia and Germany, he cabled Vice Premier Matchek in Belgrade and urged that the nation resist Hitler. When the Yugoslav army did fight and was defeated in April, he joined many others in a personal concern for a family abroad and a longing for their speedy liberation. That summer in two hectic months he wrote *Two-Way Passage*, a discussion of the factors he felt were fragmenting the nation. He closed the book with a "suggestion"—a vision of the establishment of governments for occupied countries while the war was still in progress. Staffed by Americans whose origin or heritage was that of the nation they were to govern, such bodies would help hearten the citizens of captive nations until the war ended. And once peace was restored, the temporary American "occupation" and rebuilding of liberated countries would be carried out by knowledgeable, sympathetic men who would also spread America's democratic ideals to people and governments rising from the ashes of a ruined continent. To further his "suggestion," Adamic resigned the editorship of *Common Ground* and began a newsletter titled

In Re: Two-Way Passage. He of course also developed lectures concerning his plan, calling it at times both "The Passage Back" and "ARM"—"the American Reconstruction Mission."

In January of 1942, *Two-Way Passage* suddenly brought an invitation to the Adamics for dinner with President and Mrs. Roosevelt. Adamic accepted the invitation with both professional and personal satisfaction. He speculated that his "Passage Back" might be of interest in the highest seat of government, and he felt his efforts during the past year or so had been justified to his wife. Childless and destined to remain so, Stella was a constant participant in all of his projects. But when he came to discuss the European war and wished to aid in government work, she disapproved and firmly urged that his most valuable contribution would be to continue his Nation of Nations Series. In fact, it was the consideration of her wishes rather than political factors such as the Hitler-Stalin Pact that earlier caused Adamic publicly to remain somewhat isolationist while privately he was ready for war; and had Stella not relented, he might have had a much different career during the 1940s. He designated *Two-Way Passage* the second of his Nation of Nations books, but it only barely seemed to qualify. He could now at least credit that book with his taking Stella to the White House. The invitation lifted from his shoulders, for a time, the burden of further proof.

In *Two-Way Passage*, Adamic expressed his long held distrust of Britain's influence in Europe, and in his "suggestion" had Uncle Sam tell John Bull that not England, not France, not Russia, but "only we Americans can fix up Europe." Therefore, the fact that Prime Minister Winston Churchill was also a guest at the Roosevelt's table led Adamic to wonder whether the evening's conversation might not be based on a serious discussion of his ideas. In the desperate days of early 1942 when the problems of war far outnumbered the available solutions, the episode was more than enough to encourage Adamic. He continued to foster his vision, although before long it necessarily became but one portion of his total involvement in the events of world conflict. Similarly, Washington never implemented "the Passage Back." Yet the organization of "liberation" governments proved difficult enough; and somewhere between the real officer who became the fictional Major Joppalo of John Hersey's *A Bell for Adano* and the stark political facts of postwar positions such as a High Commissioner to a divided Germany, a Supreme Allied Commander of Japan, and a dozen leaderships of Eastern European people's republics, the "suggestion" from *Two-Way Passage* remains one of the hopeful but "impossible" schemes of a decade whose history proves hardly more plausible. Furthermore, if the Kennedy years can be said to have scanned the Roosevelt years for ideas to use in the 1960s, not the least of the adaptations may be that altruistic portion of "the Passage Back" which was present in the conception of the Peace Corps.

From his experience and files and correspondence concerning acculturation, Adamic had for some time been isolating the problem of name changing; and in July of 1942 he published *What's Your Name?*, the third of his Nation of Nations books. Then he turned to the most personal of the many disruptions of American society the war had created. He cared nothing for the residue of the 1934 Belgrade regime which had bustled off to London to become the Yugoslav Government-in-Exile. Thus when the Partisan movement arose and proved both militarily effective and independent of Drazha Mikhailovich, the Royal Government's representative in the field, Adamic saw the possibility of an end to that rule which he believed had preserved itself and foreign interests rather than strive for the free development of Yugoslavia. He was little concerned that the Partisans were basically Communist in organization. The

Moscow trials of the previous decade had caused him to delete his concluding, pro-Russian remarks from all editions of *The Native's Return* after 1938; and he was hardly one of those American leftist hangers-on who were suddenly reprieved when the Nazis subdued the Balkans and attacked Russia. Yet he did hold to his basic opinion that should the Yugoslav and other Balkan peoples "overthrow their present racketeer rulers," they would then find a natural position in the Russian sphere. In addition, he trusted early information that the Partisans had widespread, non-political support and membership from among the people, and that they represented, after so many previous failures, nearly a true grassroots movement. He thus decided for the Partisans, and well before first Britain and then the United States, with perhaps different but no better rationale, did so.

In December of 1942, in the *Saturday Evening Post* and in an expanded form in the new journal *Yugoslavia*, he published the first major article in America supporting the Partisans. With that publication Adamic himself became a significant divisive force in the fragmentation of the unity he sought among citizens of Yugoslav background and between them and their fellow Americans. For the remainder of his life he would have to combat the implications of his choice, but beneath the pragmatism of his decision lay the most ambitious of his attempts "to get at the truth about things." Once it is understood that his support of the Partisans and their leader Tito was both politically anti-monarchial and idealistically an exercise of his belief that men might ultimately achieve both national and international "unity in diversity," it can then be seen that he was being completely consistent after the war when he defended Russia yet sided with an independent Yugoslavia; that he berated America because he so bitterly wanted her to be a nation he could defend; and that as the world powers, willy-nilly, juggled peoples and atomic destruction, he suffered the agonizing and private tragedy of the loss of hope.

For the next two years Adamic expended enormous energy in a variety of activities he considered necessary to the United States and the world. He helped organize and lead American Slav groups in support of both the American war effort and Tito. He was the first president of The United Committee of South-Slavic Americans and the founder and first editor of the Committee's *Bulletin*. He appeared at war bond drives, continued his own newsletter under the title *War & Post-War*, and pressed Washington for aid to Yugoslavia. In 1943 he published *My Native Land*, in which he explained the history and present crisis of the Yugoslav peoples in an attempt to increase American understanding and support. In July of 1944 he was asked to join the Yugoslav work of the Office of Strategic Services. He answered he was very willing to do so, but he stressed that he believed postwar developments in Yugoslavia would stem primarily from the People's Liberation Movement, and that unless official Washington began to accept the desirability of such developments, the OSS would probably find him of little real use. No further message came from the OSS. That October, upon learning that the Yugoslav Council of Liberation had awarded him the Order of Unity, Adamic wrote Marshal Tito: "Perhaps you are puzzled by the official behavior of the United States toward Yugoslavia. I cannot begin in a letter to explain the complexities of our vast democratic land, its great virtues and its lacks and evils."

In 1944 Adamic also continued his work on the value and extent of the ethnic variety of America. He became the general editor of *The Peoples of America Series* and for *Woman's Day* began his "They Believed in Liberty" articles, which the following year he expanded into *A Nation of Nations*, the fourth and last book of that series. But his traveling, lecturing, organizing, and writing often exhausted him and several times caused him to relinquish to others the completion of a project he had begun. When the Japanese surrendered, therefore, he was ready to rest. America and her allies had won the war, a cable informed him that all of his immediate family had survived, and Yugoslavia was to join the United Nations. Yet for Adamic it was from the start at best an uneasy peace.

Early in 1946 the Adamics received a request from Upton Sinclair to use the story of their White House visit in one of his own works.[7] The preparation of some notes for Sinclair led Adamic to write *Dinner at the White House*, a book in which the evening was clearly interpreted in the light of his disappointment in the course of events between 1942 and 1946. The world seemed full of the hatreds he had warned of in *Two-Way Passage*, and the basis of many specifics he cited was his sense of America's failure to have adopted a "democratic" foreign policy. He felt the breach between Britain and Russia probably could never be closed; but he saw no reason why the United States, the most powerful nation in the world, had not and could not now act independently. Her possession of the atomic bomb made it incumbent on her to take the lead for peace—to think in terms of "One World" rather than to perpetuate the "Either-Or" world of former days.

Although he had never been very specific about what "unity" would evolve once the "diversity" he saw in America, and then the world, came to be clearly understood by all, he said several times that America would go somewhat "Left." Still, he believed the American way was neither communism nor socialism. When publicizing the "suggestion" of his *Two-Way Passage* he had often mentioned the creation of a "true United Nations," a federated world. Late in 1942, for example, in

[7] See "Author's Note" and Chapter 8—"Much Depends on Dinner"— in Upton Sinclair, *Presidential Mission* (New York, 1947), pp. vii and 158-179 respectively.

the Zionist *The New Palestine*, he stated: "I am for a free Jewish homeland in Palestine which is not anything exclusive and separate but a part of a world organized upon the basis of an intense consciousness of all people's interdependence. I am also for a free Slovenia, a free Croatia, and a free Serbia in a free Balkan or southeast-European confederation in a free United Europe, which is part of a free World State." The fact remained, however, that he had as an alternative to extant polities no new form to offer as a solution to the social, economic, and political problems of the belief that all men are created equal. Thus partly in continuation of his hope for an evolutionary equality within the nation and among nations and partly in submission to the international politics of the East-West confrontation, in *Dinner at the White House* he stated "that American capitalism (with some changes in structure and in the thought habits of influential people) and Soviet socialism (with some changes in outlook) *could* coexist for a long time, conceivably until they leveled off into a similar way of life containing some of the best aspects of both. Each country needs a better knowledge of the other's pattern of thought and feeling." If there was no international "Middle Road for America," he remarked, there was none "even for ourselves internally. The orthodox Marxists will be proved right—that it's class against class: capitalism *versus* socialism, imperialism *versus* world revolution. We'll be compelled to fight things out on a Right-and-Left basis, here and abroad." That battle, he noted, could only lead to World War III, with America's atomic bomb playing the villain in the total ruin that would ensue.

Obviously, no small portion of Adamic's view was generated by a desire to maintain Yugoslavia. In his enthusiasm he saw that nation as a new symbol of the successful struggle of all men for freedom. And in that spirit he ignored, or excused as best he could, the one-party imperfections of Tito's Belgrade and the fact that the circumstances of Yugoslavia's past and present were unique and did not obtain in most of the other Communist territories. He believed Yugoslavia could become a bridge of understanding between the world's two great postwar powers, and he was not simply rationalizing events when he noted that "partly owing to our lack of a positive democratic orientation toward the backward countries . . . Soviet ideology has seeped into some parts of the world." This ideology filled, he believed, a vacuum between the growth of Russia's dynamism and America's stasis. He therefore desperately wanted to involve America and Yugoslavia with one another for their mutual good; America would begin to take the lead in world unity, and Yugoslavia would be given the opportunity and aid to develop. "Owing to our peculiar political history," he wrote, "only we can open the Middle Road to the future which most of the world's peoples prefer to the extreme Right and Left roads when they have an opportunity to choose."

As the United States moved toward implementation of the Truman Doctrine and the Marshall plan, and Yugoslavia executed Mikhailovich, imprisoned Archbishop Stepinac, and shot down two American planes, Adamic found it increasingly difficult to explain objectively his idea of the American-Yugoslavian interrelationship. When early in 1947 Winston Churchill successfully sued him for libel on the basis of a footnote in *Dinner at the White House*, Adamic found open only a few publications that were not specifically leftist; and indeed he expected nothing less in light of the nation's mood as he interpreted it. The more America and Russia postured, the less valid seemed his requests for tolerance and understanding at home and abroad. When after a visit to the Freedom Train in 1947 he noted that the exhibits contained too little material about the immigrant and the Negro, his criticism was judged anti-American. Organizations he led during World War II or to which he still belonged came under the scrutiny of the House Committee on Un-American Activities, and by 1948 his name began to be included in the public statements of recanting American Communists. The confessionals of Louis Budenz, for example, provided nothing about Adamic which had not already appeared in his books and articles. But few newspapers carried the full text of Adamic's candid rebuttal, and much of the country did not pursue the matter beyond the headlines. Even many of those immigrants and their families whom Adamic had for years supported to the nation as new and valuable Americans now proved themselves so well integrated that they deserted him in favor of current "American ideals." Yet by lecture and his newsletter, now titled *T & T: Trends & Tides*, Adamic continued to press home his views on national and international equality, Yugoslavia, and the corruption of America's potential. Now and again his words were sharp, his voice shrill, his logic faulty, but always in an attempt to make order of the chaos into which he believed the world had plunged.

When Henry Wallace announced his candidacy for the presidency, Adamic avidly threw in his support. To faithful friends and new, straightforward acquaintances who noted specific Communist Party activity in the Wallace camp, he answered that all beliefs had a right to participate and that the Communist numbers were needed but their power would be kept under control. In July of 1948 Adamic was appointed a member of the Progressive Party Platform Committee; and because it was obvious the Communist element was not under control, he soon convinced Wallace to pay less attention to the Left in his speeches. The Communists, Adamic warned, were interested only in recruiting as many Progressives as might come over after election day.

When the November returns came in, Adamic was hardly surprised by Truman's victory, but the failure of the Progressives to make significant gains did disappoint him. He felt the United States was now completely committed to a disaster course, and his reflections on the matter were sharpened by the fact that in June the Cominform had expelled Yugoslavia. He suspected he understood the independence of Yugoslav thought which could have forced the separation, but he could not imagine Yugoslavia's survival with both Washington and Moscow against her. In January of 1949, therefore, he went to Belgrade although, as he had said seventeen years earlier, he wanted to go to Russia as well. In later years this desire only compounded the Communist aspect of his public image; at the time he did indeed hope to reach Russia to convince someone, anyone, neither to abandon Yugoslavia nor increase world tensions. Denied a Russian visa, he settled for a visit only to Yugoslavia. Yet matters could have gone better there. He was reunited with his family and friends. He saw the marks the war had left but felt the determination in the people as well. He met with dignitaries in the new government—some of whom were old acquaintances—and he had conferences with Tito. When he questioned Moscow's actions, officials replied that they were honestly as baffled as he. However, when he tried to turn the conversation toward the methods he thought might help solve both the problems of Yugoslavia and the world, his listeners were polite but noncommittal. Perhaps no foreigner had done more for Yugoslavia than had Adamic; nevertheless, the vision he carried was presented to preoccupied minds. The Yugoslavs, standing independent and isolated, could believe only in themselves; and even that was questionable since many in the government were, though expelled, still loyal to Stalin. As Adamic typically both pressed for information about the country and argued to correct his Yugoslav hosts' views of

America, he seemed to many an agitated man from the past, a former hero whose intentions were good but whose immediate pertinence was questionable. More than a little disappointed but convinced that Tito and his nation must survive, Adamic returned home in June of 1949.

While abroad, Adamic learned that his wife was seriously ill; and he returned to the New Jersey farm to find that Stella was recuperating in California. For a month or so he lingered at Milford, arranging his affairs and working at bits of a new book. The years had taken a great deal of his energy, and his public position was enigmatic. To many Americans he was, if not an outright "Red," at least a Communist sympathizer; that he supported a Yugoslavia which was anathema to Moscow seemed not to matter. The Communists in turn berated him for both a continued pro-Jewish position on Palestine and his Titoist stand. Furthermore, Stella was now not only physically weak but also hardly sanguine about his work. Nevertheless, when he did follow her to California, they were reunited to the extent that while they lived separately, they did work together on his new book.

For the next two years the content of that volume fluctuated between a biography of Tito and a general treatment of the fallibility of modern man. Often revising and yet equally expanding the manuscript, Adamic found it difficult to ascertain a center for either his work-in-progress or his world. Russia's development of an atomic bomb seemed to make her an equal partner with the United States in the threat to the survival of mankind. He deplored the Korean conflict as the beginning of World War III, and with the Yugoslavs considered it an unchecked Communist aggression and feared that Moscow's ambitions in the Middle East might easily cause Yugoslavia again to become a battleground. Furthermore, he was subjected to criticism and threats by those who harbored, once again, historic Balkan sectional antagonisms and by those for, or against, Communism in general and Yugoslavia in particular. In what finally became a combination of almost stereotyped Slavic suspicion and an overwhelming realization of the tangle of world events, he began to fear reprisals from America, Yugoslavia, and Russia for what he did or did not write. He warned his close friends, no mattter what their beliefs, to protect themselves by staying away from him.

In the summer of 1951, with his spirit dulled but sometimes joyously telling those with whom he had to deal that his book was long and as honest as he could make it, Adamic returned alone to the farm at Milford. For the next few months he worked only fitfully. His manuscript was now of two parts—that history and discussion of Tito and Yugoslavia which his wife eventually guided into print as *The Eagle and the Roots*; and a second portion, also of book length, titled "The Big Lie," in which he reiterated his frustration at America's failure to develop for the benefit of all men. Both parts bore the characteristics of his desire for eventual world unity and clearly manifested the author's lack of conviction. Personally he saw no possibility of a new birth of freedom anywhere in the world; and in his manuscript he held out only the vestige of that ideal. His attempt "to get at the truth about things" and to make "an effort to understand them" came, finally, to be no more or less complete or satisfactory than mankind itself. On September 4, 1951, his study-garage already consumed by fire, Adamic was found lying on a bed in his burning farmhouse, a rifle angled across his thigh and a fatal bullet wound in his head. The shock, confusion, and seeming mystery of his death in great measure obscured, and continues to obscure, the fact that a life was ended for which more of the nation and world might have mourned.

Perhaps other immigrants who reached the shore of twentieth-century America made as great an effort as Louis Adamic did to understand the nature and role of their new nation, but it is doubtful that he had any rival in his effort to convey that attempt to a popular audience. As even the most random selection of the readings listed here will make clear, Adamic never altered his basic desire to learn and explain; and even had that desire made him less than correct, it would have led him into events and conflicts which we now know are crucial to a full appraisal of the decades in which he lived. Throughout his life, in relations with intellectuals espousing theories, he kept himself a critical and often more knowledgeable observer; but before the unique potential he saw in his adopted America he stood an equally confirmed idealist who wanted a nation, and if possible the world, to be a work of art.

His early investigations of himself and his new country established his view "that America was a Land Nobody Knew"; and his compulsion as an observer-writer caused him to aspire to the role of an "earnest, objective socio-political-cultural" Darwin "who would get busy in the vast Sargasso Sea that was America." He could not investigate without attempting to guide, and there he was nagged by the realization that men could not for long be legislated into using their better natures, and yet would hardly exercise such natures consistently if left alone. He avoided what he called the "shortcuts" of Marxism and other radical means of change for America, but elsewhere he saw such means as at least a partial step toward freedom. His interest in the enunciated liberties of Russia, however, was no greater than his interest in those of the United States. He was equally disappointed by the failure to truly implement those liberties in either country, although he spent more effort on America's shortcomings because he was an American writer and believed America more than any other nation had progressed, and still could progress, further along the road of true democracy. The production of his lifetime, therefore, bears the stamp of both the man and the United States; and the study of any single piece of that production raises numerous questions about both.

One may ask, for example, as did a Pittsburgh *Press* editorial during World War II, whether American Slavs and their descendants, and as well those of other immigrant stock, should not have ignored events in their places of heritage because they were American citizens; but in so wondering, one may have to ask whether and how the United States could have done so. Or one may seek to discover whether it is the personality of the author or the truth of his observations that causes Adamic's native born hero of *Grandsons* to write: "I was too closely tied up with contemporary America. I carried my death in me all the time." To be pondered too is the continuing validity, or "relevance," to use a current word, of Adamic's opinions concerning the United States as "a nation of nations." The concept was reargued during the political maneuvers necessary for the revision of the immigration laws in the early 1960s, and the Whitman phrase itself appears as the first chapter title of President John F. Kennedy's *A Nation of Immigrants*.[8] One could take note of the rise of the Black and other minority movements and recall Adamic's belief in a balance between the pride an individual racial group should have in its unique diversity and its unity and usefulness as a group within a whole society. The advent of the prefix *Afro* might well have jogged the memory that Adamic hoped for something better than the hyphenated American; and the reader is not certain he is handling a book thirty years old when he discovers in *Two-Way Passage*: "For one thing, the Indians 'invaded' Washington carrying signs like: 'WHY DON'T YOU ALL GO BACK, YOU DERN FURRINERS? LET THE BUFFALO GRAZE AGAIN!'" There is

[8] New York, 1964.

something contemporary in these lecture remarks from 1936: "I plead that education should begin producing people whose values will be *qualitative* and not quantitative . . . people who will know and *feel* that, lest humanity perish, men must cease spending most of their energy scheming how to harm one another, how to fight one another, and begin looking toward a goal, toward ideals, toward something they wish to become and make of the world."

It should, then, come as no surprise that during Adamic's lifetime portions of his work were included in anthologies of the kind which perpetually offer readers contemporary civilization, current issues, or America-in-profile; or that in the sixties his work began to appear in anthologies designed to evaluate for the uninitiated the 1930s or the contributions of the foreign born; or that more recently the Arno Press-New York *Times* would reprint *Laughing in the Jungle* for inclusion in The American Immigration Collection; and that Chelsea House-Vintage would, with cover quotations from both H. Rap Brown and Philip Roth's *Portnoy's Complaint*, reprint *Dynamite* for the Cherry Pie Series on violence in America. It is not so much that either America or Adamic has cycled as it is that beneath the widely varying surface detail of Adamic's prose is the continuing study of the human condition. His canon, therefore, provides sufficient provocation for both his, and our, day.

I. Periodicals

1 "Rešitev zastavice v št. 11. Drevo. Adamič Alojzij, dijak v Ljubljani" and "Odgovor na šaljivo vpranšanje v st. 11. Prav so rešili: Adamič Alojzij," *Angelček: Priloga "Vrtcu,"* XVIII (December 1, 1910), 191, 192. Adamic's winning solution to the November word puzzle.

1a *Vrtec,* XL (December 1, 1910), 200.

2 Trans. "Simple Martin," by Ivan Cankar, *The Living Age,* CCCXI (December 24, 1921), 773-775.

3 Trans. "The Burden of Authority," by Pisal Pugelj, *World Fiction,* I (February, 1922), 87-91.

3a *Prosveta,* December 22, 1926, p. 6.

4 Trans. "Two Churches," by Milan Ogrizovic, *The Living Age,* CCCXIII (April 22, 1922), 232-237.

4a Richard Eaton, ed., *The Best European Short Stories of 1928* (New York: Dodd, Mead, 1929), pp. 226-236.

5 Trans. "*Slovenski Narod,*" a portion of "A Week of the World" section, *The Living Age,* CCCXIII (April 22, 1922), 254.

6 A. Henri (pseud.), "The Mutineer," *Pearson's Magazine,* XXXXVIII (April, 1922), 32-33.

6a "The Mutiny," *Overland Monthly*, LXXXIV (December, 1926), 386.

7 "An Amateur Athlete," *The Open Road*, IV (April, 1922), 39.

8 Trans. "At the Tailor's Dance," by S. H., *The Living Age*, CCCXIII (June 24, 1922), 786-790.

9 Trans. "In the Department of Public Order," by Ivan Krnic, *The Living Age*, CCCXIV (July 15, 1922), 167-171.

10 "The Yugoslav Royal Wedding," from *Slovenski Narod*, *The Living Age*, CCCXIV (July 29, 1922), 292-293.

11 Trans. "A Cup of Coffee," by Ivan Cankar, *Overland Monthly*, LXXX (July, 1922), 22-23.

11a *Juvenile: Monthly Magazine for Young Slovenians in America*, a portion of *Mladinski List*, V (March, 1926), 82-83.

11b *Juvenile . . . Mladinski List*, XIV (July, 1935), 214-215.

12 Trans. "The Montenegrin Widow," by Zofka Kveder, *The Living Age*, CCCXIV (August 26, 1922), 541-546.

12a *Prosveta*, January 19, 1927, p. 6; January 26, p. 6.

13 Trans. "The Religion of My Boyhood," by Milan Ogrizovic, *The Living Age*, CCCXIV (September 2, 1922) 600-605.

13a "God," *Golden Book Magazine*, V (June, 1927), 841-844.

14 Trans. "The Horrified Yugoslav," a portion of "Life, Letters, and the Arts" section, *The Living Age*, CCCXV (October 14, 1922), 119-120.

15 Trans. "Betwixt Two Worlds," by Mirko Jurkic, *The Living Age*, CCCXV (October 28, 1922), 239-241.

16 A. Henri (pseud.), " 'Eyes right,' " *Pearson's Magazine*, XXXXVIII (October, 1922), 33-38.

17 Trans. "Gulsa: Tale of a Life in Bosnia," by Omer B. Mlemovich, *Overland Monthly*, LXXX (October, 1922), 48-49.

18 Trans. "Petrograd and Moscow," by I. Zupančič, *The Living Age*, CCCXVI (January 13, 1923), 85-88.

19 Trans. "The Camp Fire," by Vitomir F. Jellenc, *The Living Age*, CCCXVI (January 27, 1923), 237-239.

20 Trans. "A Yugoslav Sculptor," from *Cas*, *The Living Age*, CCCXVI (February 3, 1923), 307-308.

21 Trans. "Land Hunger," by Lovro Kuhar, *The Living Age*, CCCXVI (February 17, 1923), 417-425.

22 Trans. "Mishko," by R. Medek, *The Living Age*, CCCXVII (April 17, 1923), 51-53.

23 Trans. "Social Customs in Belgrade," by Ivan Dolenec, *The Living Age*, CCCXVII (June 16, 1923), 643-645.

24 Trans. "Stephan Raditch," by M.C.A., *The Living Age*, CCCXVIII (July 21, 1923), 112-114.

25 Trans. "Superman," by J. S. Machar, *The Living Age*, CCCXVIIII (December 8, 1923), 467-473.

26 Trans. "Our Daily Bread," by Fr. S. Finzgar, *Our World*, IV (December, 1923), 29-35.

27 Trans. "Builders," by Alojz Kraigher, *The Living Age*, CCCXX (February 2, 1924), 225-228.

27a *Prosveta*, September 22, 1926, p. 6.

28 Trans. "Strategy," by J. S. Machar, *The Living Age*, CCCXXI (May 17, 1924), 955-959.

29 Louis Adams (pseud.), "Mr. Hughes Debates," *The Truth Seeker*, October 18, 1924, pp. 666-667.

30 Trans. "Angelo the Stonecutter," by Vladimir Nazor, *The Living Age*, CCCXXIII (November 29, 1924), 483-488.

31 Trans. "The Old Fogies' Club," by Iso Velikanovich, *The Living Age*, CCCXXIV (January 31, 1925), 260-265.

32 "Young Intellectual Objects," Los Angeles *Times*, July 26, 1925, pt. 3, p. 30.

33 Trans. "An Honest Thief," by J. S. Machar, *The Living Age*, CCCXXVII (November 21, 1925), 412-415.

34 "Los Angeles—A Christian City," *Haldeman-Julius Monthly*, III (December, 1925), 55-61.

35 "Aimee McPherson's Great Faith Factory," *Haldeman-Julius Monthly*, III (January, 1926), 153-164.

36 Trans. "The Wolf," by Anton Novačan, *Juvenile: Monthly Magazine for Young Slovenians in America*, a portion of *Mladinski List*, V (February, 1926), 51-53.

37 "Mrs. Elsie Lincoln Benedict—Archpriestess of Inspirational Bunk," *Haldeman-Julius Monthly*, III (March, 1926), 401-406.

38 Trans. "Spring," by Maria Kmetova, *Mladinski List*, V (April, 1926), 123-124.

39 Trans. "Yerney's Justice," by Ivan Cankar, *Prosveta*, May 19, 1926, p. 6; and p. 6 of each of these dates: May 26; June 2, 9, 16, 23, 30; July 7, 14, 21, 28; August 4, 11, 18, 25; p. 5 of September 1, and p. 6 of September 8 and 15.

40 Trans. "At Dawn," by Ivan Cankar, *Juvenile: Monthly Magazine for Young Slovenians in America*, a portion of *Mladinski List*, v (May, 1926), 145-147.

40a *Juvenile . . . Mladinski List*, xiv (October, 1935), 314-316.

41 "Long Beach, California—Yokel's Paradise," *Haldeman-Julius Monthly*, iii (May, 1926), 649-654.

42 "Trash and Garbage on the Newsstands," *Haldeman-Julius Monthly*, iii (May, 1926), 684-690.

43 Trans. "Her Picture," by Ivan Cankar, *Juvenile: Monthly Magazine for Young Slovenians in America*, a portion of *Mladinski List*, v (June ,1926), 176-177.

43a *Juvenile . . . Mladinski List*, xiv (May, 1935), 145-146.

44 "Otoman Zar-Adusht Ha'nish, America's Master Charlatan," *Haldeman-Julius Monthly*, iv (June, 1926), 109-120; (July), 60-72.

45 Trans. "Flies," by Ivan Cankar, *The Stratford Magazine*, i (July, 1926), 3-10.

46 "The Crusader," *The American Parade*, i (July, 1926), 51-77.

46a "Križar," *Prosveta*, October 1, 1926, p. 4; October 2, p. 4; October 4, p. 4; October 5, p. 4; October 7, p. 4; October 8, p. 4. Translated by I[van] M[olek].

47 "The Mystery of Aimee Semple McPherson," *Haldeman-Julius Monthly*, IV (July, 1926), 113-119.

48 "Aimee Semple McPherson's Hoax of the Century," *Haldeman-Julius Monthly*, IV (August, 1926), 3-9.

49 "Los Angeles, Past and Present," *Haldeman-Julius Monthly*, IV (August, 1926), 39-47.

50 "Aimee Semple McPherson's Fight with Satan," *Haldeman-Julius Monthly*, IV (September, 1926), 17-28.

51 Trans. "Comedy of Justice" [Simen Sirotnik], by Ivan Cankar, *Prosveta*, October 6, 1926, p. 6; and p. 6 of each of these dates: October 13, 20, 27; November 3, 10, 17, 24; December 1, 8, and 15.

52 "The Cat That Catches the Rat," *The Open Forum*, III (October 9, 1926), 1.

53 "Was Aimee McPherson's 'Shack' in the Grove of Aphrodite?" *Haldeman-Julius Monthly*, IV (October, 1926), 17-25.

54 "The Latest Aimee McPherson Hoax," *Haldeman-Julius Monthly*, IV (November, 1926), 8-14.

55 "The Morons of Los Angeles," *Haldeman-Julius Monthly*, IV (November, 1926), 33-38.

56 Review of James Stevens, *Brawnyman*. "Brawnyman Writes a Book," *The Open Forum*, III (December 25, 1926), 2, 4.

57 Trans. "Begali," by Ivan Zorec, *Prosveta*, December 29, 1926, p. 6; January 5, 1927, p. 6; January 12, p. 6.

58 "Aimee McPherson's Trial—An Orgy of Obscenity," *Haldeman-Julius Monthly*, V (December, 1926), 22-29.

59 "Roger Baldwin Visits Los Angeles: An Evangelist of Liberty in the City of Revivals," *Haldeman-Julius Quarterly*, I (January, 1927), 150-151.

60 "Theodore Dreiser: An Appreciation—He Looks at Life Honestly, Calmly, Sympathetically, Helplessly," *Haldeman-Julius Quarterly*, I (January, 1927), 93-97.

61 Trans. "In Front of the Wine-House," by Ivan Cankar, *Prosveta*, February 2, 1927, p. 6; February 9, p. 6; February 16, p. 6.

62 "Katherine Tingley, Theosophical Boob-Baiter of San Diego," *Haldeman-Julius Monthly*, V (February, 1927), 49-69.

63 Trans. "Comes and Goes," by Anton Novačan, *Prosveta*, April 27, 1927, p. 6; May 4, p. 6.

64 "George Edwin Burnell—'Savior of the Rich,' " *Haldeman-Julius Monthly*, VI (August, 1927), 33-38.

65 "The Great Public Secret in Los Angeles," *Haldeman-Julius Weekly*, September 10, 1927, pp. 3-4.

66 "Cecil DeMille—Movie Evangelist," *Haldeman-Julius Monthly*, VI (October, 1927), 3-7.

67 "Upton Sinclair—A Prophet of Red Dawn," *The Open Forum*, IV (November 26, 1927), 1-2.

67a "Upton Sinclair—glasnik rdeče zarje," *Ameriški družinski koledar*, III (Chicago: Jugoslovanska delavska tiskovna družba, 1929), pp. 130-132.

68 "The Bright Side of Los Angeles," *Haldeman-Julius Monthly*, VI (November, 1927), 17-25.

69 "The Yugoslav Speech in America," *American Mercury*, XII (November, 1927), 319-321.

70 "Paganism in Los Angeles," *Haldeman-Julius Monthly*, VII (December, 1927), 94-97.

71 "Hollywood Movie 'Bibles,'" *Haldeman-Julius Monthly*, VII (January, 1928), 101-104.

72 "Michael Pupin—'From Inventor to Evangelist,'" *Haldeman-Julius Monthly*, VII (February, 1928), 104-113.

72a "M. Mihajlo Pupin—iznajditelj in pridigar," *Pod lipo*, IV, 5 (1928), 71-74. Translated by I[van] M[olek].

73 "The Word of Satan in the Bible: Christians Rightly Regard Ecclesiastes Suspiciously," *Haldeman-Julius Quarterly*, II (April–May–June, 1928), 3-15.

74 "The Gospel of Jesus According to Henri Barbusse," *The Open Forum*, V (June 2, 1928), 1; (June 9), 2.

75 "Bohunks," *American Mercury*, XIV (July, 1928), 318-324.

75a *Prosveta*, July 3, 1928, p. 7; July 11, p. 7.

76 "Dean Inge—An Honest Churchman," *Haldeman-Julius Monthly*, VIII (July, 1928), 78-81.

77 "Music and the Masses: Symphony Concerts as a Community Interest in Los Angeles," *Haldeman-Julius Quarterly*, II (July–August–September, 1928), 39-47.

78 "The Nation's Backbone," *Birth Control Review*, X (August, 1928), 252-253; (September), 282, 289. First section erroneously labeled as the second section of this story.

79 "Will Hays—Ignorant and Dishonest," *Haldeman-Julius Monthly*, VIII (August, 1928), 49-55.

80 "Case History," *American Mercury*, XV (November, 1928), 287-296 .

80a "Lenard Podgornik," *Prosveta*, November 7, 1928, p. 7; November 14, p. 7; November 28, p. 7; December 5, p. 7.

80b "Clovek s dušo" [The Man with a Soul], *Ljubljanski Zvon*, LII (May, 1932), 267-273; (June), 328-335. From *Laughing in the Jungle*.

80c "Eine Kroatin in Kalifornien," *Morgenblatt—Jahrbuch*, Vol. VII (Zagreb, 1933), pp. 41-47. Translated by L. M[attersburger].

81 "Superman," *American Mercury*, XV (December, 1928), 438-449.

82 "Louis Adamič," *Pod lipo*, IV, 6 (1928) 95.

83 "Robinson and Una Jeffers: A Portrait of a Great American Poet and His Wife," *The San Franciscan*, III (March, 1929), 16, 29.

84 "Land of Laughs," *American Mercury*, XVI (April, 1929), 480-487.

85 "Post-Mortems," *The Open Mind*, May 4, 1929, p. 2.

86 Review of D. H. Lawrence, *Pansies*. "Pagan and Sunward," *The Open Forum*, VI (August 10, 1929), 3.

87 "Organized Labor and the Army," *The Open Forum*, VI (October 26, 1929), 1.

88 "Prosperous America—Dressed Up, No Place to Go: Happiness a Rare Quality in Nation Where Material Wealth Has Been Exalted to the Ideal End," *The New Leader*, November 23, 1929, p. 4.

89 "Liberals in Los Angeles," *Plain Talk*, v (December, 1929), 684-691.

90 "Why Tom Mooney Stays in Prison," *The New Leader*, March 22, 1930, p. 4; March 29, p. 4.

91 "A Bohunk Woman," *American Mercury*, xix (March, 1930), 281-286.

91a *South Slav Herald*, July 1, 1932, p. 3; July 16, p. 5. From *Laughing in the Jungle*.

91b "Zena iz Dalmacije," *Ljubljanski Zvon*, lii (September, 1932), 523-532. Translated by Griša Koritnik.

91c "Zena iz Dalmacija," *Srpski književni glasnik*, N.S. xxxvii, 4 (1932), 245-255. Translated by T[one] P[otokar]. Cyr.

91d "Zena iz Dalmacije," *Jugoslavenski list*, xvi, 24 (1933), 4; 25, 4; 26, 4; 27, 4. From *Laughing in the Jungle*.

91e *Slovak Democrat* (New York), July 15, 1933, pp. 5, 10.

91f "La virino el Dalmatuju," *La Suda Stelo*, iii, 4-5 (1934), 53-56; 6-7 (1934), 69-70.

92 "Philippine Interlude," *Plain Talk*, vi (March, 1930), 303-308.

92a "Kralj Lukaš" [King Lucas], *Modra ptica*, iii (1931–1932) 257-263. Translated by Griša Koritnik.

92b "Philippinisches Zwischenspiel," *Der Wiener Tag*, June 17, 1932. Translated by L. M[attersburger].

93 Trans. "The Cow," by Fr. S. Finzgar, *Catholic World*, CXXXI (April, 1930), 71-76.

94 "The Enigma," *American Mercury*, XX (May, 1930), 68-79.

94a Edward J. O'Brien, ed., *The Best Short Stories of 1931* (New York: Dodd, Mead, 1931), pp. 3-23.

94b "Uganka," *Ljubljanski Zvon*, LII (January, 1932), 14-18; (February), 66-71; (March), 136-144. Translated by O. Skerlj.

95 "Voltaire from Kansas," *Outlook and Independent*, CLV (June 25, 1930), 282-285, 314-316. *See also* "Mr. Adamic Replies," (August 27, 1930), 679.

96 "Los Angeles! There She Blows!" *Outlook and Independent*, CLV (August 13, 1930), 562-565, 594-597.

97 "The Man with the Big Head," *Plain Talk*, VII (August, 1930), 183-192.

98 "Racketeers and Organized Labor," *Harper's Magazine*, CLXI (September, 1930), 404-416.

98a *Reader's Digest*, XVIII (December, 1930), 676-678.

99 "The 'Assassin' of Wilson," *American Mercury*, XXI (October, 1930), 138-146.

99a "The Assassin of Wilson," *New Yorker Volkszeitung (Sonntagsblatt)*, October 19, 1930, pt. II, p. 15; October 26, p. II, p. 15.

100 "Virginians on Strike," *New Republic*, LXV (December 24, 1930), 163-164.

101 "Racketeers," *New Republic*, LXV (January 7, 1931), 210-212.

102 Review of Carey McWilliams, *The New Regionalism in American Literature*. "Provincial Literature of U.S. Recognized as a Hopeful Sign," New York *Telegram*, January 9, 1931, p. 9.

102a "Literary Regionalism," *Contempo*, I (September 15, 1931), 1-2.

103 Reviews of Grace Hutchins, *Labor and Silk*; Robert W. Dunn, *Labor and Automobiles*; Anna Rochester, *Labor and Coal*; and Jack Hardy and Robert W. Dunn, *Labor and Textiles*. "Series by Radicals Deals Truthfully with Labor," New York *Telegram*, January 16, 1931, p. 7.

104 Review of J. A. Hobson, *Rationalization and Unemployment*. "Hobson Views Wants of Man as Illimitable," New York *Telegram*, January 23, 1931, p. 7.

105 "Radicalism, Ltd.: Suppression of Communist and Similar Movements Has Resulted in 'Individual Revolutions' of Sabotage by Discontented Workers," New York *World* (Editorial Section), January 25, 1931, p. 1.

106 "Louis Adamic," in George Britt's column "Behind the Backs of Books and Authors," New York *Telegram*, January 27, 1931, p. 7.

107 "Sabotage," *Harper's Magazine*, CLXII (January, 1931), 216-228.

107a "Ameriška sabotaža," *Jutro* (Ljubljana), XIII, 188 (1932), 6.

107b *Glasilo Kranjsko-Slovenske Katoliške Jednote* (Cleveland), XVIII, 35 (1932), 5.

107c Charles W. Thomas, ed., *Essays in Contemporary Civilization* (New York: Macmillan, 1931), pp. 106-128.

107d Dudley C. Gordon and Vernon R. King, eds., *College Readings on Today and Its Problems* (New York: Oxford, 1933), pp. 43-62.

108 Review of Frank H. Cushing, ed. and trans., *Zuni Folk Tales*. "Zuni Folk Tales Again Available in Cushing Book," New York *Telegram*, February 12, 1931, p. 11.

109 Reviews of Claudius J. Murchison, *King Cotton Is Sick*, and G. T. Swenning, ed., *Management Problems*. "Cotton Industry Viewed as Chaotic Without Profit to Capital, Labor," New York *World-Telegram*, March 18, 1931, p. 26.

110. " 'Ghosts'—Homeless Man's Symbol for America," New York *World-Telegram*, March 19, 1931, p. 23.

110a *Prosveta*, September 2, 1931, p. 8.

111 "Machine Guns to Solve Unemployment Problem," New York *World-Telegram*, March 19, 1931, p. 30.

112 Review of Louis Colman, *Lumber*. "Life Tale of Toiler Has Vigor: Novel of Working Class in Sawmill Story," New York *World-Telegram*, April 8, 1931, p. 28.

113 Review of Richard T. Ely, *Hard Times: The Way In and the Way Out*. "Hard Times Suggest New Book," New York *World-Telegram*, April 15, 1931, p. 30.

114 Review of Stanley B. Mathewson, *Restrictions of Output Among Unorganized Workers*. "Why Men 'Soldier' Described in Study," New York *World-Telegram*, April 22, 1931, p. 36.

115 "Mr. Adamic Replies," *New Freeman*, III (April 22, 1931), 137-138.

116 Review of Tom Tippett, *When Southern Labor Stirs.* "Gastonia Land," New York *Herald Tribune*, April 26, 1931, Sec. XI, p. 19.

117 "Louis Adamic Has Arrived," Carbondale *Leader* (Pennsylvania), April 28, 1931, p. 1.

118 "Tragic Towns of New England," *Harper's Magazine*, CLXII (May, 1931), 748-760.

118a Don Congdon, ed., *The Thirties: A Time to Remember* (New York: Simon and Schuster, 1962), pp. 37-48.

118b Milton Meltzer, *Brother, Can You Spare a Dime? The Great Depression: 1929–1933* (New York: Alfred Knopf, 1969), pp. 23-24, 63-64.

119 "Adamic Defends 'Tragic Towns,' " New York *World-Telegram*, May 15, 1931, p. 27.

120 "Dynamite Explained," *Contempo*, I (June, 1931), 1, 3-4.

121 "Mr. Adamic Writes," Scranton *Times* (Pennsylvania), July 9, 1931.

122 "Dear Tom O'Flaherty," *Contempo*, I (July, 1931), 2.

123 Review of Sarah Gertrude Millin, *The Sons of Mrs. Aab.* "The First Reader," New York *World-Telegram*, August 20, 1931, p. 23.

124 Review of Dean Stiff [Nels Anderson], *The Milk and Honey Route: A Handbook for Hobos.* "Ex-Bum," *The Survey*, LXVI (September 15, 1931), 563.

125 "Can Business Acquire Social Conscience?" *Labor Age*, XX (September, 1931), 15-19, 26.

125a *Prosveta*, November 4, 1931, p. 8; November 11, p. 8; November 18, p. 8; November 25, p. 8; December 2, p. 8.

126 "Study in Contrasts," New York *World-Telegram*, October 3, 1931, p. 18.

127 Anon. Review of Margaret Whipple, *The Kirbys*. "Adventures of a Babbitt Family," New York *World-Telegram*, October 7, 1931, p. 28.

128 Review of Sherman H. M. Chang, *The Marxian Theory of the State*. "Books on Review," *Contempo*, I (October 15, 1931), 3.

129 "On Our Discontents," New York *Sun*, October 17, 1931, p. 33.

130 "Dog Robber," *Liberty*, VIII (October 24, 1931), 42-45.

131 "Too Many Breadlines," *Commonweal*, XIV (October 28, 1931), 625-627.

132 "The Land of Promise: An Immigrant of 1913 Looks at America in 1931," *Harper's Magazine*, CLXIII (October, 1931), 618-628.

132a *Prosveta*, September 30, 1931, p. 8; October 7, p. 8; Octobber 14, p. 8; October 21, p. 8; October 28, p. 8.

132b "Zemlja obecanja. Doseljenik iz 1913, gleda na Ameriku od 1931," *Amerikanski Srbobran Kalendar: 1932* (Pittsburgh, 1932), pp. 54-73. Translated by Ivan Mladineo. Cyr.

133 Review of Sherwood Anderson, *Perhaps Women*. "Perhaps It's Nonsense," *Contempo*, I (November 1, 1931), 1.

134 Review of Labor Research Association, *Labor Fact Book.* "Labor 'Fact' Book," *Contempo,* I (November 15, 1931), 2.

135 Reviews of John D. Hicks, *The Populist Revolt,* and John McConaughty, *From Cain to Capone.* "Revolts and Rackets," *Contempo,* I (December 1, 1931), 1, 4.

136 "Louis Adamic's Retort," *Contempo,* I (December 15, 1931), 1-2.

137 Review of B. A. Botkin, *Folk-Say: A Regional Miscellany.* "A New Work from Oklahoma," New York *World-Telegram,* December 16, 1931, p. 26.

138 "The Collapse of Organized Labor," *Harper's Magazine,* CLXIV (January, 1932), 167-178.

139 "The Papers Print the Riots," *Scribner's Magazine,* XCI (February, 1932), 109-111.

140 "Symbol," *Pagany,* III (Spring, 1932), 135-143.

141 Review of Dreiser Committee, *Harlan Miners Speak: Report on Terrorism in the Kentucky Coal Fields, Compiled by the Dreiser Committee.* "Coal War," New York *Herald Tribune,* April 17, 1932, Sec. XI, p. 21.

142 "Bogataši—begunci" [Rich Men—Fugitives], *Prosveta,* July 25, 1932, p. 3.

142a *Ponedeljski Slovenec,* V, 25 (1932), 4.

142b "Runaways," *The American Spectator,* July, 1933, p. 2.

143 "Američan v svoji stari domovini," *Ljubljanski Zvon,* LII (July–August, 1932), 444-466.

143a "Home Again from America," *Harper's Magazine*, CLXV (October, 1932), 513-528.

143a* "My Home-Coming to Slovenia," *South Slav Herald*, November 1, 1932, p. 2; "Louis Adamich Describes Meeting His Family After Nineteen Years," p. 4; Odyssey of a Yugoslav: Louis Adamič Continues His Story," November 16, p. 3; "The Odyssey Ends," p. 5; "Homecoming to Yugoslavia: Louis Adamič Continues His Story," December 1, p. 5; "A Feast for the Prodigal: Louis Adamič Ends His Homecoming Story," December 16, p. 4.

143b "Jedan emigrant obilazi svoju postojbinu. Od Luja Adamiča," *Vreme*, XII, 3879 (1932), 1-2; 3880, 2; 3881, 2; 3882, 4; 3883, 2. Cyr.

143c "Home Again in Carniola," *Scholastic*, XXIV (April 7, 1934), 4-7. From *The Native's Return.*

143d "Povratek v domovino," *Slovenski poročevalec*, XII, 212 (1951). Translated by Ivan Crnagoj. From *The Native's Return.*

144 "Kriza ameriškega individualizma" [The Crisis of American Individualism], *Ljubljanski Zvon*, LII (July–August, 1932), 385-402. Translated by G[riša] Koritnik.

144a "The Passing of American Individualism," *American Scholar*, I (October, 1932), 423-429.

144b "Najnovejša dejstva o krizi v Ameriki," *Ponedeljski Slovenec*, V, 40 (1932), 1-2.

144c "Razvoj američkog individualizma," *Književnik* (Zagreb), VI (January, 1933), 10-15. Translated by [Branko] Kojic.

144d "Kriza američkog individualizma," *15 dana*, III (July, 1933), 196-197. From *Ljubljanski Zvon* above.

144e "The Passing of American Individualism," *Reference Shelf*, IX (January, 1935), 78-86.

145 Review of Georges Duhamel, *Prizori iz bodočega zivljenja* (Oton Zupančič's Slovenian translation of *Scènes de la Vie Future*). *Ljubljanski Zvon*, LII (July–August, 1932), 505-506.

146 "Clarence Darrow: The Portrait of a Great Actor," *National Spotlight*, n.v. (August, 1932), 12-14.

146a "Clarence Darrow: A Great Actor," *Reader's Digest*, XXI (September, 1932), 65-67.

147 "The Next War," *Nation*, CXXXV (October 5, 1932), 310.

148 "Crkva u Mexiku" [Church in Mexico], *Književnik* (Zagreb), V (December, 1932), 445-447. Written especially for *Književnik*. Translated by B[ranko] Kojic.

148a "Slovenski kmetje molijo za mehiško cerkev" [Slovenian Peasants Pray for Mexican Church], *Novi čas*, I (December, 1932), 3.

148a* *Književnost*, I (January, 1933), 29-31.

149 Review of John S. Gambs, *Decline of the I.W.W.* "A Book About the I.W.W.," *Contempo*, III (January 10, 1933), 6.

150 Review of Božidar Jakac, *Odmevi rdeče zemlje*. "Božidar Jakac: *Odmevi rdeče zemlje*," *Sodobnost*, I (January, 1933), 32-34. Translated by S[tanko] Leben.

151 "Wedding in Carniola," *Harper's Magazine*, CLXVI (January, 1933), 170-180.

151a *Prosveta,* January 11, 1933, p. 8; January 18, p. 8; January 25, p. 8; February 1, p. 8.

151b "A Wedding in Our Village," *South Slav Herald,* February 1, 1933, p. 2; "Courtship in a Yugoslav Arden: Louis Adamic Continues His Description—of Slovene Nuptials," February 16, p. 3; "A Slovene Bride Is Led Home: Louis Adamic's Narrative Continued from Last 'Herald' Issue," March 1, p. 4; "Wine, Feasting—and Song: Louis Adamic Ends His Story of a Slovene Village Wedding," March 15, p. 3.

151c "Zenidba u Kranjskoj," *Novo doba* (Split), XVI, 29 (1933), "prilog," 1-2. Translated by I. F. Lupis-Vukic.

152 "Louis Adamič o Ameriki nekoč in zdaj" [Louis Adamic about America Then and Now], *Prosveta,* February 23, 1933, p. 3; February 24, p. 3. Edited by M[ilo] K[lopčič].

153 "Ljubezen v Ameriki" [Love in America], *Ljubljanski Zvon,* LIII (February, 1933), 89-101. Translated by Olga Grahor. A portion of "The Darkened Plain," later titled *Grandsons.*

153a *Prosveta,* March 2, 1933, p. 4; March 3, p. 4; March 6, p. 4.

154 "Pogovor" [The Conversation], *Sodobnost,* I (February, 1933), 59-70. Translated by M. Leben. A portion of "The Darkened Plain," later titled *Grandsons.*

155 "Slučaj Mooney-Billings" [The Mooney-Billings Frame-Up], *Književnost,* I (February, 1933), 54-58, 87-90. From *Dynamite.*

156 "Business," *Sodobnost,* I (March, 1933), 119-123. Translated by M[arija] Leben. A portion of "The Darkened Plain," later titled *Grandsons.*

157 "Luj Adamič o američkim knjigma" [Louis Adamic about American Books], *Nova Evropa*, XXVI (March, 1933), 129-130; (July), 315-317; (September), 420-424. Cyr. and Lat.

158 "Statement by Louis Adamic at the American Consulate in Zagreb, Yugoslavia, on February 20, 1933," *Prosveta*, April 11, 1933, p. 1.

159 "Letter from Yugoslavia," *Saturday Review of Literature*, IX (May 27, 1933), 620.

159a "L. Adamicevo pismo. Louis Adamič o jugoslavenskoj književnosti i književnicima," *Novo doba* (Split), XVI,144 (1933), 2.

159b "Louis Adamič o M. Krleži," *Književni horizonti*, I, 1 (1934), 30.

160 "Sacco in Vanzetti," *Književnost*, I (June, 1933), 206-214. From *Dynamite*.

161 "A Letter from Louis Adamic," *Prosveta*, July 26, 1933, p. 6.

161a "Adamič bo pisal o Jugoslaviji. Objavil bo serijo člankov v ameriških revijah in jih pozneje izdal v knjigi kot celoto. Adamičevo pismo in pojasnilo javnosti o njegovem delu in stališču," *Prosveta*, July 26, 1933, p. 4.

162 "Mesto v zraku" [A City Suspended in Space], *Sodobnost*, I (August, 1933), 341-349; (September), 403-410. Translated by S[tanko] Leben.

162a *Prosveta*, November 16, 1933, p. 4; November 17, p. 4; November 18, p. 4; November 21, p. 4.

163 "One Hundred Million Peasants: Will the 'Green International' Revive in the Balkans?" *New Republic*, LXXVI (September 13, 1933), 119-122.

163a *Prosveta*, October 4, 1933, p. 8; October 11, p. 8.

164 "Smeh v džungli. Avtobiografija ameriškega priseljenca" [*Laughling in the Jungle*], *Prosveta*, September 29, 1933, p. 4; and p. 4 of each of these dates: October 2, 3, 5, 6, 9, 10, 12, 13, 16, 17, 19, 20, 23, 24, 26, 27, 28, 31; November 2, 3, 6, 7, 9, 10, 13, 14, 16, 17, 18, 21, 23, 24, 25, 28; December 1, 4, 5, 7, 8, 11, 12, 14, 15, 18, 19, 21, 22, 26, 28, 29; (1934) January 2, 4, 5, 8, 9, 11, 15, 16, 18, 19, 22, 23, 25, 26, 29, 30; February 1, 2, 5, 6, 8, 9, 12, 13, 15, 16, 19, 20, 22, 23, 26, 27; and March 1, 2, 5, 6, and 8. Translated by Stanko Leben.

165 "Vobliji" [The Wobblies], *Književnost*, I (September, 1933), 329-339. From *Dynamite*.

166 Trans. "What It Means To Be a Communist in Yugoslavia," by "a young Communist" [Edvard Kardelj], *New Masses*, IX (September, 1933), 3-8.

166a "White Terror: A Case History," *New Republic*, LXXVI (August 16, 1933), 6-7.

166b "Borba," *Borba* (Toronto), April 21, 1936, p. 2; April 23, p. 2; April 25, p. 2; April 28, p. 2; April 30, p. 2; May 2, p. 2; May 5, p. 2; May 7, p. 2; May 9, p. 2.

167 "Silver Candlesticks," *The Outlander*, No. 4 (Fall, 1933), 24-35.

168 "A Letter from Louis Adamic," *Prosveta*, October 4, 1933, p. 8.

168a "Adamičevo pismo," *Prosveta*, October 4, 1933, p. 3.

169 "Adamic's View on Labor Literature," *Prosveta*, October 18, 1933, p. 8.

170 Review of Calvin B. Hoover, *Germany Enters the Third Reich*. "Ameriška knjiga o Hitlerju" [American Book about Hitler], *Sodobnost*, I (October, 1933), 478-479.

171 "Dalmatia," *Hrvatska* (Chicago), November 2, 1933, p. 1.

172 "Analiza Jugoslavije," *Novi Svijet*, November 25, 1933, pp. 1, 4.

173 "Bedni otroci v Ameriki" [Poor Children in America], *Ljubljanski Zvon*, LIII (November, 1933), 660-665. Translated by Olga Grahor. A portion of "The Darkened Plain," later titled *Grandsons*.

174 "Belgrade—Boom Town of the Balkans," *Travel*, LXII (November, 1933), 18-22, 43-44.

174a "Adamič opisuje Belgrad," *Prosveta*, November 9, 1933, p. 4.

174b *Prosveta*, November 15, 1933, p. 8.

174b* *Hrvatski Glas*, November 23, 1933, p. 3.

174c "This Miracle of Belgrade," *South Slav Herald*, February 17, 1934, p. 3.

174d *Jugoslavija*, V, 1 (1934), 8-9.

175 "Death in Carniola," *Harper's Magazine*, CLXVII (November, 1933), 693-704.

175a *Prosveta*, October 25, 1933, p. 8; November 1, p. 8; November 8, p. 8.

175b "Smrt u Kranjskoj," *Pregled* (Sarajevo), VIII, knj. X, 121 (1934), 32-37; 122 (1934), 93-102. Translated by D. Bugarski. Cyr.

175c "Smrt u Kranjskoj," *Novo doba* (Split), XIX, 305 (1936), 12-14. Translated by I. F. Lupis-Vukic.

175d "Smrt čeka ujka Janeza," *Vreme*, XX, 6703 (1940), [Literary Supplement, 1]. Cyr.

175e Frank H. McCloskey and Robert B. Dow, eds., *A Pageant of Prose* (New York and London: Harper, 1935), pp. 209-222.

175f "Death Waits for Uncle Yanez," *Reader's Digest*, XXXVI (February, 1940), 107-110.

176 "Sta je liberalizam?" [What Is Liberalism?], *Književnik* (Zagreb), VI (November, 1933), 451-453.

177 "Mr. Guggenheim and I Become a Legend in Yugoslavia," *The Sunday Review of The Brooklyn Eagle*, December 3, 1933, pp. 10-11.

177a "Mr. Guggenheim in jaz—v slovenski legendi," *Prijatelj*, XII (August, 1938), 290-292. Translated by Joža Glonar. From *The Native's Return*.

178 "Letter from Louis Adamic," *Enakopravnost* (Cleveland), December 20, 1933.

179 "A Letter from Louis Adamic," *Enakopravnost* (Cleveland), December 23, 1933.

180 "An Immigrant's America," *American Magazine*, CXVI (December, 1933), 52-53, 82, 84. One of the "This Is My America" series of the *American Magazine*.

180a "Naseljenčeva Amerika" *Enakopravnost* (Cleveland), December 21, 1933, Sec. II, pp. 1, 2.

180b Elmer R. Smith, ed., *Meet an American!* (New York and Chicago: Harcourt, Brace, 1944), pp. 96-105.

181 "Dalmatia—A Peasant Riviera," *Travel*, LXII (December, 1933), 24-28, 42, 44.

182 "The King Business in the Balkans," *Yale Review*, XXIII (Winter, 1933), 330-350.

183 "Kako u Americi književnik postaje prekonoc milionar" [How a Writer Becomes Rich Overnight in America], *Pozorište*, n.v., 19 (1933), 339. Cyr.

184 "Ponos. (Moj najljepši doživljaj u Dubrovniku)" [The Pride. (My Most Beautiful Experience in Dubrovnik)], *15 dana*, III, 4 (1933), 58-59. The conversation of Louis Adamic "stylized" by H[ijacint] P[etris]. Adamic stated publicly that this interview never took place.

184a *Novo doba* (Split), XVI, 47 (1933), "prilog," 3.

185 Review of Ivan Molek, *Veliko mravljišče*. "Molek Continues the Story of Tone Plesec," *Prosveta*, January 3, 1934, p. 8.

186 "Sons of the Black Mountain," *Travel*, LXII (January, 1934), 26-30, 47-48.

187 "Torture in Belgrade," *New Masses*, X (March 6, 1934), 21.

188 Review of Roman Dyboski, *Poland*. "Pilsudski's Poland," *New Republic*, LXXVIII (March 28, 1934), 193-194.

189 "They Always Come Back," *Woman's Home Companion*, LXI (March, 1934), 12-13.

190 "Who Built America? Profiteers, Professionals Patriots or 'Vile Immigrants,'" *Common Sense*, III (April, 1934), 13-15.

190a "Kdo je zgradil Ameriko?" *Enakopravnost* (Cleveland), April 26, 1934, p. 2.

190b *Nova Doba* (Cleveland), May 9, 1934, p. 6.

190c "Kdo je zgradil Ameriko?" *Nova Doba* (Cleveland), May 16, 1934, p. 6.

190d *Enakopravnost* (Cleveland), May 19, 1934, p. 2.

190e "Otvorena useljenička reč Americi," *Nova Evropa*, XXVII (September, 1934), 325-330. Translated by I[vo] F. L[upis]-V[ukic]. Cyr.

191 "Keeping the Lid on the Balkans," *Current History*, XL (May, 1934), 149-156.

192 "The Steel Strike Collapses," *Nation*, CXXXIX (July 4, 1934), 9-13.

193 "Company Unions and the A. F. of L.," *Nation*, CXXXIX (July 18, 1934), 67-69.

194 "Where We Stand—A Symposium: Louis Adamic," *International Literature*, No. 3 (July, 1934), 82.

195 "Strange Strike in Jugoslavia," *Nation*, CXXXIX (August 29, 1934), 239-240.

196 "Yugoslav Writer Predicted Alexander's Assassination," New York *World-Telegram*, October 9, 1934, p. 1.

197 "King a 'Gangster,' Adamic Charges," New York *Evening Post*, October 10, 1934, pp. 1, 3.

197a "King Was a Tyrant, Louis Adamic Holds," New York *Times*, October 10, 1934, p. 17.

197b "Louis Adamic Describes King As Deft Actor," New York *Herald Tribune*, October 10, 1934, p. 4.

198 "Adamic Amused at Newspaper's Charge He's 'Red,' " New York *Post,* October 13, 1934, p. 2.

199 "What Next in Jugoslavia?" *Nation*, CXXXIX (October 24, 1934), 470-471.

200 "The Native's Return," *Book of the Week Club Supplement of* Philadelphia *Record*, November 18, 1934, pp. 1-19. The Fiction Editor of the *Record* noted this abridgement of *The Native's Return* was "the first non-ficition book ever run as the Book of the Week." The Sunday book "Supplement" was a weekly syndication, liberally edited, in various newspapers. This Adamic item also appeared, for example, in *The Knickerbocker Press* (Albany), November 18, 1934, pp. 1-16, and *The Oregon Journal*, November 25, 1934, pp. 1-19.

201 "Thirty Million New Americans," *Harper's Magazine*, CLXIX (November, 1934), 684-694.

201a "Kolmekymmentä Miljoonaa Uus-Amerikalaista," *Raivaaja* (Fitchburg, Massachusetts), May 8, 1936, p. 2; May 9, p. 2; May 11, p. 2; May 12, p. 2; May 13, p. 2.

201b "30 milionov novoamerikancev," *Obzorja*, II (June, 1939), 243-248; "Poglavje iz knjige 'Moja Amerika,' " III (January, 1940), 31-37; (February), 81-85. Translation by Vito Kraigher. From *My America*.

201c Arno L. Bader and Carlton F. Wells, eds., *Essays of Three Decades* (New York: Harper, 1939), pp. 220-236.

201d Willard Thorp, Merle Curti, and Carlos Baker, eds., *American Issues*, I (Philadelphia: Lippincott, 1941), p. 785-789.

201e J. Hooper Wise, et al., eds., *The Meaning in Reading* (New York: Harcourt Brace, 1943), pp. 363-374.

202 "What the Proletariat Reads," *Saturday Review of Literature*, XI (December 1, 1934), 321-322.

202a *Golden Book*, XXI (February, 1935), 182-186.

202b Erich A. Walter, ed., *Essay Annual: A Yearly Collection of Significant Essays, Personal, Critical, Controversial, and Humorous* (Chicago: Scott, Foresman, 1935), pp. 213-221.

203 Review of Leon Dennen, *Where the Ghetto Ends: Jews in Soviet Russia*. "Jews in the U.S.S.R.," *Nation*, CXXXIX (December 5, 1934), 655.

204 "Američki pisac Luj Adamič o sebi, o Južnoj Srbiji, o Americi itd" [American Writer Louis Adamic about Himself, South Serbia, America, Etc.], *Vardar*, III, 266 (1934), 3-4. Cyr.

205 "Louis Adamič za naše i ostale iseljenike" [Louis Adamic for Our and Other Immigrants], *Jadranski dnevnik*, I, 14 (1934), 3.

206 "The Great 'Bootleg' Coal Industry," *Nation*, CXL (January 9, 1935), 46-49.

206a *Reader's Digest*, XXVI (March, 1935), 39-42.

206b "Velika industrija tihotapskega premoga," *Modra ptica*, XI (February, 1940), 65-73. Translated by Vito Krajger. From *My America*.

207 Review of Edward Corsi, *In the Shadow of Liberty*. "An Immigrant Who Made Good in America," New York *Herald Tribune*, January 27, 1935, Sec. VII, p. 3.

208 "A Communication," *Jewish Frontier*, II (January, 1935), 20.

209 "Hill-Billies Come to Detroit," *Nation*, CXL (February 13, 1935), 177-178.

210 "LaFollette Progressives Face the Future," *Nation*, CXL (February 20, 1935), 213-215.

211 "A Talk with Phil LaFollette," *Nation*, CXL (February 27, 1935), 242-245.

212 "Will Rubber Snap?" *Nation*, CXL (March 20, 1935), 334-336.

213 "The Ilinois Miners' War Goes On," *Nation*, CXL (March 27, 1935), 361-362.

214 Review of Sherwood Anderson, *Puzzled America*. "A Puzzled American," *Saturday Review of Literature*, XI (April 13, 1935), 621.

215 Review of Karl Billinger, *Fatherland*. "Agony under Fascism," *Nation*, CXL (April 17, 1935), 457-458.

216 Review of Stoyan Christowe, *Heroes and Assassins*. "Macedonians, Ever Warriors," New York *Herald Tribune*, May 5, 1935, Sec. VII, p. 2.

217 Review of Jack Conroy, *A World to Win*. "Nothing to Lose," *Saturday Review of Literature*, XII (May 11, 1935), 14.

218 "My Friend in Herzegovina," *Woman's Home Companion*, LXII (June, 1935), 14-15, 36, 40, 42, 45-46.

218a "Moj prjatelj Hercegovac" in *Radnički crveni Kalendar: 1936* (Zagreb, 1936), pp. 26-39.

218b *The American Slav*, (November, 1938); (December); (January, 1939). From *My America*.

219 Review of Erskine Caldwell, *Some American People.* "Erskine Caldwell's Social Criticism," *Saturday Review of Literature*, XIII (November 9, 1935), 10.

220 "Foreigners Are News in Cleveland: The Story of an Interesting Journalistic Experiment," *Interpreter Releases* (Foreign Language Information Service), XII, no. 52, Series E; Interpreter Report No. 9 (November 22, 1935), 416-419.

220a *Reader's Digest*, XXXIII (August, 1938) 71-72. From *My America.*

220b " 'Tujci' so novost za Cleveland," *Edinost* (Maribor), February 15, 1940, pp. 2-3. Translated by Vito Kraigher.

221 "Sarajevo—Mustafa's Home Town," *Rotarian*, XLVIII (January, 1936), 34-36, 69-73. From *The Native's Return.*

222 Review of Bertita Harding, *Royal Purple.* "Bucket of Blood," *New Republic*, LXXXV (February 5, 1936), 374.

223 "Shall We Send Them Back to Hitler?" *Nation*, CXLII (March 25, 1936), 377-378.

224 "Education on a Mountain," *Harper's Magazine*, CLXII (April, 1936), 516-530.

224a *Reader's Digest*, XXVIII (June, 1936), 23-27.

224b "Education En La Montaña," *Ultra* (Havana), IV (October, 1936), 299-302.

224c William H. Cordell and K. C. Cordell, eds., *American Points of View* (Garden City, New York: Doubleday, Doran, 1937), pp. 260-286.

224d "Black Mountain: An Experiment in Education," *HIKA* (Kenyon College), VIII (October, 1940), 2-4, 16-32. From *My America.*

225 "Harry Bridges: Rank and File Leader," *Nation*, CXLII (May 6, 1936), 576-580.

226 "Cherries Are Red in San Joaquin," *Nation*, CXLII (June 27, 1936), 840-841.

227 "Candidate for the Honor Roll," *Nation*, CXLIII (July 25, 1936), 111.

228 Et al. "The Western Writers' Conference," *New Republic*, LXXXVIII (September 23, 1936), 185.

229 Reviews of Henry David, *The History of the Haymarket Affair*, and Edward Dean Sullivan, *This Labor Union Racket*. "History and Hysteria," *Saturday Review of Literature*, XIV (September 26, 1936), 10.

230 ". . . but People Are Good!" *Mid-Week Pictorial: The Newspicture Weekly*, October 10, 1936, pp. 24-25.

231 "Louis Adamic's Reply," *Saturday Review of Literature*, XIV (October 10, 1936), 11.

232 "Who Killed the King?" *Nation*, CXLIII (October 10, 1936), 417-418.

233 "Why I Wrote the 'Cradle of Life,' " *Mid-Week Pictorial: The Newspicture Weekly*, October 24, 1936, pp. 22-23.

233a *Prosveta*, November 4, 1936, p. 7.

233b "Louis Adamič: Zašto sam napisao 'Zipku života,' " *Novo doba* (Split), December 14, 1936, p. 2.

234 "Pittsburgh," *Pacific Weekly*, November 9, 1936, p. 301.

235 "Aliens and Alien-Baiters," *Harper's Magazine*, CLXXIII (November, 1936), 561-574.

235a "Ulkomaalaiset Ja Ulkomaalaissyöjät," *Raivaaja* (Fitchburg, Massachusetts), January 5, 1937, p. 2.

236 "Sitdown," *Nation*, CXLIII (Decemzer 5, 1936), 652-654; "Sitdown: II," (December 12, 1936), 702-704.

237 "The Sitdowns," *Nation*, CXLIII (December 5, 1936), 688.

238 Review of Cecil Carnes, *John L. Lewis, Leader of Labor.* "John L. Lewis as Phenomenon," *Nation*, CXLIII (December 12, 1936), 708.

239 "Harry Bridges Comes East," *Nation*, CXLIII (December 26, 1936), 753.

240 "The Man with the Wooden Leg," *Westways (Formerly Touring Topics)*, XXIX (February, 1937), 14-15.

241 "John L. Lewis' Push to Power," *Forum and Century*, XCVII (March, 1937), 131-137.

241a "Problemi Amerike. (Sta hoce John L. Lewis?)," *Nova Evropa*, XXX (July–August, 1937), 254-262.

241b "Problemi Amerike. (Sto hoce John L. Lewis?)," *Svijet* (New York), XXVI, 9534 (1937), 2; 9536, 2.

241c Covjek o kojem govori cijela Amerika. John L. Lewis pokrenuo je milijune američkih radnika," *Danica*, 26 (1937), 11.

242 Review of Nexhmie Zaimi, *Daughter of the Eagle.* "A Glowing Portrait of an Ancient People," *Saturday Review of Literature*, XVI (June 19, 1937), 12.

243 "Jack Raper, Cleveland's Best Citizen," *Nation*, CXLV (July 10, 1937), 42-45.

243a "Louis Adamic Calls Raper 'Most Successful Citizen,'" *The Cleveland Press*, July 8, 1937, pp. 1, 17 or 19 of Sec. II.

244 "Kolijevka života. Odlomak iz romana" [Cradle of Life. Fragment from the novel], *Književnik* (Zagreb), X (August–September, 1937), 321-332. Translated by Branko Kojic.

244a "Zibelka življenja," *Zenski svet*, XVI, 2 (1938), 29-33. Translated by O[lga] G[rahor].

245 "A Steel Man OK's the C.I.O.," *Nation*, CXLV (November 27, 1937), 582-585.

246 "The Truth about the C.I.O.," *Forum and Century*, XCVIII (November, 1937), 232-237.

247 Review of Joseph Henry Jackson, *Notes on a Drum: Travel Sketches in Guatemala*. "A Tour of Guatemala," New York *Herald Tribune*, December 5, 1937, Sec. X, p. 18.

248 Review of Geoffrey and Kit Bret Harte, *Island in the Sun*. "New Books," *Saturday Review of Literature*, XVII (December 11, 1937), 20.

249 "Pogledi na savremeni svijet" [Views of the World Today], *Jadranski dnevnik*, IV, 55 (1937), 11.

250 Review of Fred E. Beal, *Proletarian Journey*. "To Russia and Back," *Saturday Review of Lieterature*, XVII (January 1, 1938), 19.

251 Review of William Seabrook, *These Foreigners*. "New Books," *Saturday Review of Literature*, XVII (March 28, 1938), 21.

252 "The Millvale Apparition," *Harper's Magazine*, CLXXVI (April, 1938), 476-486.

252a *Reader's Digest*, XXXII (May, 1938), 5-9.

252b " 'Sablasti' u hrvatskoj crkvi u Millvaleu. Neobičan doživljaj hrvatskog slikara Maksimilijana Vanke u Americi," *Jutarnji list* (Zagreb), XXVII, 9439 (1938), 24.

252c Philip Van Doren Stern, *The Midnight Reader: Great Stories of Haunting and Horror* (New York: Holt, 1942), pp. 406-429.

253 "My America: Louis Adamic," *American Prefaces*, III (April, 1938), 97-112. Preview of *My America.*

253a "From My Diary for 1931," *American Prefaces*, V (June, 1940), 135-136.

254 " 'Hello Phil': Belgrade and Madison: Symbols of Two Ways of Life," *Common Sense*, VII (May, 1938), 16-19.

254a "Halo Phil!" *Obzorja*, III (April–May, 1940), 189-196. Translated by Vito Krajger.

255 Review of Faith Baldwin, *Rich Girl, Poor Girl.* "New Books," *Saturday Review of Literature*, XVIII (June 25, 1938), 19.

256 Reviews of Ethel Hueston, *High Bridge*, and Kathleen Norris, *Heartbroken Melody.* "New Books," *Saturday Review of Literature*, XVIII (July 2, 1938), 20, 21.

257 Reviews of Margaret C. Banning, *You Haven't Changed*; Maud Diver, *The Dream Prevails*; Sophie Kerr, *Adventures with Women*; Olive H. Prouty, *Lisa Vale*; and Barbara B. Stephens, *The Strangest Son.* "New Books," *Saturday Review of Literature*, XVIII (July 9, 1938), 20.

258 Review of Allis McKay, *Woman about Town.* "New Books," *Saturday Review of Literature*, XVIII (July 30, 1938), 21-22.

259 "Ingrates at Yaddo," *Esquire*, x (July, 1938), 75, 180-184.

260 Review of Margaret Widdeman, *Hand on Her Shoulder.* "New Books," *Saturday Review of Literature*, XVIII (August 27, 1938), 21.

261 "America's 'Left' Gropes for a Way Out," *The New Leader*, September 3, 1938, p. 3.

262 Review of Fannie Cook, *The Hill Grows Steeper.* "New Books," *Saturday Review of Literature*, XVIII (September 17, 1938), 21.

263 Reviews of Bradford Smith, *American Quest*, and Dawn Powell, *The Happy Island.* "American Don Quixote" and "New Books," *Saturday Review of Literature*, XVIII (September 24, 1938), 11, 20.

264 "Moj Amerika: Ce je človek iz dveh svetov . . ." [My America: On Being of Two Worlds], *Ljubljanski Zvon*, LVIII (September–October, 1938), 463-473. Translated by Olga Grahor. From *My America.*

264a* *Slovenija* (Ljubljana), VIII, 1 (1939), 2.

264b *Obzornik*, VI, 9 (1951), 552-562.

265 Review of Faith Baldwin, *Hotel Hostess.* "New Books," *Saturday Review of Literature*, XVIII (October 1, 1938), 20.

266 Review of Wessel Smitter, *F.O.B. Detroit.* "Men and Machines," *Saturday Review of Literature*, XIX (November 5, 1938), 6.

267 "An Appeal from Louis Adamic: To the Croatian Immigrants in the U.S. and Their American-born Children and Grandchildren," *Hrvatski Svijet*, November 12, 1938, p. 2. A typical newspaper printing of Adamic's "Broadside."

268 Review of Margaret C. Banning, *Too Young to Marry*. "New Books," *Saturday Review of Literature*, XIX (December 10, 1938), 18.

269 Review of P.R. Barnes, *Crum Elbow Folks*. "New Books," *Saturday Review of Literature*, XIX (December 17, 1938), 20.

270 "My America," *Omnibook*, I (December, 1938), 1-104. Abridged *My America*.

271 "Plymouth Rock and Ellis Island," *American Prefaces*, IV (December, 1938), 46-48. From *My America*.

272 "Making Them Feel at Home," *Rotarian*, LIV (February, 1939), 12-15.

272a " 'Grenak je tujine kruh. . . .' Kaj piše američki slovenski pisatelj Adamič o naših izseljencih" [Bitter Is the Bread of a Foreign Country. . . . What the Slovenian-American Writer Adamic Says about Our Immigrants], *Slovenec*, LXVII, 40 (1939), 5.

272b "Stranci u Americi. Pučanstvo američkih gradova. Louis Adamič o problemu stranaca u USA" [Foreigners in America. Hostility of American Cities. Louis Adamic about the Problem of Foreigners in U.S.A.], *Hrvatski list* (Osijek), XXI, 115 (1940), 12.

273 ". . . war will be easy; to stay out, hard," *Survey Graphic*, XXVIII (February, 1939), 152. A portion of Adamic's letter answering "The Challenge to Democracy Reaches over Here: What Can Americans Do About It: How and Where Can We Take Hold?"

273a " 'Calling America.' Mišljenje Louisa Adamiča," *Nova riječ*, IV, 158 (1939), 14.

274 "The Making of Americans," *Current History*, L (March, 1939), 17-19.

274a "Our Citizenship Factories," *Reader's Digest*, XXXIV (March, 1939), 48-51.

274b Asher N. Christensen and E. M. Kirkpatrick, eds., *Running the Country: An Anthology of American Politics in Action* (New York: Holt, 1946), pp. 201-207.

275 "Adamic Asks Workers' Aid for New Book," *The New Leader*, April 8, 1939, p. 8.

276 "Request for Information and Opinion," *Scholastic*, XXXIV (April 29, 1939), 4T.

276a "Plymouth Rock and Ellis Island," *Humanity*, I (November, 1939), 24.

277 "Free Ad for an Author," *Evening Sun* (Baltimore), May 4, 1939, p. 4.

278 "Reply to an Answer to an Ad," *Evening Sun* (Baltimore), May 17, 1939, p. 4.

279 "Manifesto," *Nation*, CXLVIII (May 27, 1939), 626. Adamic among the signers of this document representing the Committee for Cultural Freedom.

280 Review of Carey McWilliams, *Factories in the Fields*. "The Jig Is Up," *Saturday Review of Literature*, XX (July 22, 1939), 6.

281 "Questions for American Jews," *National Jewish Monthly*, LIII (July–August, 1939), 385, 397-398.

282 Review of Pietro di Donato, *Christ in Concrete*. "Muscular Novel of Immigrant Life," *Saturday Review of Literature*, XX (August 26, 1939), 5.

283 "Request for Facts and Views," *North Georgia Review*, IV (Early Autumn, 1939), 57-59, 62-63.

284 "The New America," *FLIS Press Releases*, Index No. 4806 (October 2, 1939), 1-2.

285 "The Woman from Croatia," *Saturday Evening Post*, CCXII (October 21, 1939), 41-42, 44, 46.

286 "L. Adamic Endorses Novak's Dictionary," *Prosveta*, October 25, 1939, p. 8.

287 "Družinsko življenje v gospodarski krizi" [Family Life and the Depression], *Obzorja*, II (November–December, 1939), 500-508. Translated by Vito Kraigher. From *My America.*

287a "Družinsko življenje v Ameriki v căsu krize (1930–1932)," *Naša žena* (Ljubljana), XI, 1 (1952), 12-15.

287b "Family Life and the Depression" in Harvey Swados, ed., *The American Writer and the Great Depression* (New York: Bobbs, Merrill, 1966), pp. 200-218.

288 "They Came from Pomerania," *Saturday Evening Post*, CCXII (December 9, 1939), 35-36, 81-82, 84.

289 "An Important Appeal to Hungarian Youth! From Louis Adamic: To the Hungarian Immigrants," *Református Ujság* (1939), 14-15.

290 "Plymouth Rock and Ellis Island: Summary of a Lecture by Louis Adamic," *Nova Doba* (Cleveland), January 17, 1940, p. 7.

290a *Scholastic*, XXXVI (February 12, 1940), 11-13.

290b *The American Slav*, G. (March, 1940), 7-11, 18-20, 22. A reprinting of the Common Council for American Unity pamphlet.

291 " 'New Deal' me kliče" [The New Deal Calls Me], *Edinost* (Maribor), January 25, 1940, p. 3; February 1, pp. 2-3. Translated by V[ito] K[raigher]. From *My America.*

292 "Yugoslavia's Democratic and Liberal Tradition Lives in the Memory of King Peter," *American-Yugoslav Reflector*, I (January, 1940), 10.

293 "Just Who Are We Americans?" *San Francisco Teachers Bulletin*, XXII (February, 1940), 6-7, 22, 26-27; (March).

294 Review of A. Nakashian, *A Man Who Found a Country*. "Armenian Horse and Buggy Doctor," *Saturday Review of Literature*, XXII (May 4, 1940), 12.

295 "Posedanje in hitra rast C.I.O." [The Sitdown and the Swift Growth of the C.I.O.], *Ljubljanski Zvon*, LX (May–June, 1940), 285-290; (July–August), 388-395. Translated by Vito Kraigher. From *My America.*

296 Review of Benjamin Appel, *The People Talk*. "American Humanity on Parade," *Saturday Review of Literature*, XXII (June 8, 1940), 5.

297 "The Old Alien by the Kitchen Window," *Saturday Evening Post*, CCXIII (July 6, 1940), 27, 39-40, 45-46.

297a "Star priseljenec ob kuhinjskem oknu," *Ljubljanski Zvon*, LX (September–October, 1940), 506-512; (November–December), 605-609. Translated by Vito Kraigher.

298 " 'Bodoča vojna': diktature in Amerika" ["The Next War" and Fascism, and America], *Obzorja*, III (August, 1940), 331-336; (September–October), 384-387. Translated by Vito Kraigher. From *My America.*

299 "Our Country." The fourth of twenty-four articles titled "Our Country" written exclusively for the NEA Service (official title became Newspaper Enterprise Association Inc. in 1962) by twenty-four "of the nation's most famous authors." The national syndication date was generally September 12, 1940, e.g., Sheboygan *Press*, p. 2, or New York *World-Telegram*, p. 22, which listed Adamic as "third" in the series.

300 "Editorial Aside," *Common Ground*, I (Autumn, 1940), 2, 103.

301 "This Crisis Is an Opportunity," *Common Ground*, I (Autumn, 1940), 62-73.

301a "Bigness or Bigotry?" in Robert M. Bartlett, ed., *Discovery: A Guidebook for Living* (New York: Association Press, 1941), pp. 77-79.

302 "From Bohemia: Ma and Pa Karas,"*Survey Graphic*, XXIX (October, 1940), 489-494. From *From Many Lands.*

302a *Woman's Day* (July, 1941), 22-23, 61-62, 64-66. Second in a series of *Woman's Day* stories by Adamic. *See below* no. 311.

302b " 'Ma' a 'Pa' Karasovi," *Amerikán Národní Kalendár: 1942* (Vol. LXV) (Chicago: Augusta Geringera, 1942), pp. 52-64. Translated by J. V. Welcl.

303 "Judge All by What They Do, Not Who They Are," a part of "Americans vs. Fifth Columnists: *A Symposium,*" *Survey Graphic*, XXIX (November, 1940), 548-549.

304 "Training in Fraternity," *Childhood Education*, XVII (November, 1940), 102.

305 "Greek Immigration in U.S.," *Commonweal*, XXXIII (January 31, 1941), 366-368.

306 Review of Carl Wittke, *We Who Built America. Harvard Educational Review*, XI (January, 1941), 148-150.

307 "Adamic Urges Resistance: Author Calls on Yugoslavia to Give Battle to Hitler," New York *Times*, March 16, 1941, p. 27.

307a "Louis Adamic's Appeal to Dr. Vlatka Mačeka," *Glas naroda*, March 20, 1941, p. 2.

308 "And Proud of It," *This Week Magazine*, March 16, 1941, p. 2.

308a *Reader's Digest*, XXXVIII (June, 1941), 86-88.

309 "Foreign Ports," *National Parent-Teacher*, XXXV (March, 1941), 4-6.

310 "Address by Louis Adamic: Author and Editor of Common Ground," *Interpreter Releases*, XVIII, Series E (April 7, 1941), 133-135.

311 "A Woman of Courage," *Woman's Day* (April, 1941), 20-21, 56-59. First in a *Woman's Day* series titled "Americans in the Making."

312 "From Many Lands," *Omnibook*, III (April, 1941), 34-66. Abridged *From Many Lands*.

313 "Opportunity in Crisis," *Rotarian*, LVIII (May, 1941), 14-15, 64-66.

314 "The St. Paul Festival of Nations," *Common Ground*, I (Summer, 1941), 103-110.

315 "The Importance of Being Yourself," *This Week Magazine*, August 17, 1941, p. 2.

315a "I'm Glad I'm Kobotchnik Again," *Magazine Digest*, XXV (December, 1942), 103-106. From *What's Your Name?*

315b "The Man and His Dog," *Canadians All*, II (Spring, 1944), 5, 47.

315c "The Importance of Being Kobotchnik," *Fraternal Outlook*, IX (November, 1947), 8, 20-21.

316 Review of Rebecca West, *Black Lamb and Grey Falcon: A Journey Through Yugoslavia*. "Journey Through Yugoslavia," *Saturday Review of Literature*, XXIV (October 18, 1941), 5, 31.

316a *The Bulletin of the United Committee of South-Slavic Americans*, III (January–February, 1945), 7-8.

317 Review of Martin Gumpert, *First Papers*. "American Discovery," *Saturday Review of Literature*, XXIV (November 1, 1941), 6.

318 "Two-Way Passage," *Saturday Review of Literature*, XXIV (November 8, 1941), 13.

319 "Goebbels Was Cock-Eyed!!" *Sunday Herald* (Bridgeport, Connecticut), December 28, 1941, p. 23. "Number One of 'We Are All Americans' Series."

320 Louis Adamic's notice of withdrawal as editor. *Common Ground*, II (Winter, 1942), 2.

321 "There Can Be No 'V' for Victory Without 'U' for Unity," *Sunday Herald* (Bridgeport, Connecticut), January 11, 1942, p. 9.

322 "America in the 1840's," *National Jewish Monthly*, LVI (January, 1942), 152-153, 163.

323 "December 7, 1941 and T-WP," "Mrs. Roosevelt and a Catholic Nun," "A Blast from Samuel Grafton," "Dorothy Thompson and Vera Michels Dean," "The Nature of Our Current Unity," "Preparedness," "From a German American," and "Brief Notes," *In Re: Two-Way Passage*, I (January, 1942), 1-4.

324 "Doctor Alice and Doctor Ted," *Woman's Day*, (January, 1942), 12-13, 56-58, 62-63.

325 "Tolerance Is Not Enough," New York *Times*, February 15, 1942, Sec. VII, p. 38.

326 "Two-Way Passage," *Omnibook*, IV (February, 1942), 65-96. Abridged *Two-Way Passage*.

327 "T-WP in the White House," "Is the T-WP 'Suggestion' Already in Use?" "Governments-in-Exile," "How Do I Know?" and "Need of Preparedness for Victory," *In Re: Two-Way Passage*, I (February, 1942), 1-4.

328 "Za mir je treba delati sedaj" [To Have Peace We Have to Fight Now], *Cankarjev glasnik*, V (February, 1942), 146-148.

329 "Was It Worth While?" *This Week Magazine*, March 29, 1942, p. 2.

330 "T-WP and Morale" and "A Personal Note," *In Re: Two-Way Passage*, I (March, 1942), 1-2, 4.

331 "Raymond Moley Is Worried," *In Re: Two-Way Passage*, I (April, 1942), 1-2.

332 "Our Leadership Needed: Louis Adamic Thinks Mrs. Roosevelt's Remarks on 'The American Way' Were Misunderstood," New York *Herald Tribune*, May 31, 1942, Sec. II, p. 9.

333 " 'You Want Some Sense to It,' " *In Re: Two-Way Passage*, I (May, 1942), 1.

334 "Training for Postwar Work," "The Passage Back," and "Concepts Underlying T-WP," *In Re: Two-Way Passage*, I (June, 1942), 1-3.

335 "Talk in a Blackout," *This Week Magazine*, July 26, 1942, p. 2.

336 "A Week in Washington" and "Stirrings in Universities and Colleges," *In Re: Two-Way Passage*, I (July, 1942), 1-3.

337 "Talk in a Taxi," *This Week Magazine*, August 23, 1942, p. 2.

338 "American Teachers for Eastern Europe and the Balkans," "Pearl Buck Wants to Use the Japanese Americans," and "Shall We Speculate a Little?" *In Re: Two-Way Passage*, I (August–September, 1942), 1-2, 3.

339 "Names," *Common Ground*, III (Autumn, 1942), 21-26.

340 "The Passage Back," *Yugoslavia*, I (October 1, 1942), 3.

341 Et al. "Negroes Also Have Feelings," New York *Times*, October 20, 1942, p. 20.

341a *In Re: Two-Way Passage,* I (November–December, 1942), 1, 2.

342 "Sincerely Yours: A Correspondence: Louis Adamic and Others," *Contemporary Jewish Record,* V (October, 1942), 466-477.

343 "No Hyphens This Time," New York *Times,* November 1, 1942, Sec. VII, pp. 18, 38.

344 "After Victory—What?" *This Week Magazine,* November 8, 1942, pp. 4-5.

344a *Scholastic,* XLI (December 7-12, 1942), 14-15.

344b *Congressional Record: Proceedings and Debates of the 77th Congress,* Second Session, Appendix, Vol. LXXXVIII, pt. 10 (Government Printing Office: Washington, D. C., 1942), pp. A4242-4244. Remarks of Emanuel Celler, December 10, 1942.

345 " 'ARM' oder 'Wie die Nachkriegswelt wieder aufgebaut werden Kann,' " *Reconstruction: Aufbau* (New York), November 20, 1942, p. 4.

346 "Palestine, Britain, and America," *The New Palestine,* XXXIII (November 20, 1942), 6-13.

347 "Why Don't They Change Their Names?" *Saturday Evening Post,* CCXV (November 28, 1942), 76.

348 "Partizani and Mihajlovic" [The Partisans and Mikhailovich], *Cankarjev glasnik,* VI (November, 1942), 95-106.

348a *Njiva,* VI, 8 (1942–1943), 4-14.

349 "The Future Requires Faith—Now!" *Motive: Magazine of the Methodist Student Movement,* III (November, 1942), 21-22.

350 "Just a Beginning," "The Worst Is Yet to Come," and "The American Reconstruction Mission," *In Re: Two-Way Passage*, I (November–December, 1942), 1, 2.

351 "Then Came the Nazis. . . ," *This Week Magazine*, December 13, 1942, p. 2.

352 "Mikhailovitch: Balkan Mystery Man," *Saturday Evening Post*, CCXV (December 19, 1942), 20-21, 84, 86.

353 "Obey Your Heart," *Junior League Magazine*, XXIX (December, 1942), 2-3.

354 "Can Writers Believe in the Future?" *Saturday Review of Literature*, XXVI (January 2, 1943), 3-4, 19.

355 "Adamic, Noted Slavs Here Greet Yugoslav Liberation Government," *Daily Worker*, January 20, 1943, p. 2. A message of greeting to Ivan Ribar, President of the Constituent Assembly in the territories newly liberated by the People's Liberation Army of Yugoslavia; message released from Adamic's home.

355a "Zlatko Balokovic, Frano Petrinovic i dr. Ugledne ličnosti šalju pozdrav Narodnom vijecu Jugoslavije," *Novosti* (Toronto), III, 303 (1943), 1.

356 "Are You Thinking of Changing Your Name?" *Good Housekeeping*, CXVI (January, 1943), 37, 68.

357 "Carriers of Freedom," *Educational Method*, XXII (January, 1943), 152-156.

358 "The Appointment of Gov. Lehman," "Developments in Colleges and Universities," "Postwar Work for the Middle-Aged," "Conscientious Objectors," "Need of an Unofficial Board," "Why People in Immigrant Groups Must Be Used," and "Institute on Eastern and Central Europe," *In Re: Two-Way Passage*, II (January, 1943), 1-4.

359 "Again: The Worst Is Yet to Come," "Expediency and Improvisation Will Not Be Enough," "Notes on the State Department," and "For the Record: On the Yugoslav Situation," *In Re: Two-Way Passage*, II (February–March, 1943), 4-8.

360 " 'America' Is a Magic Name," *Journal of Educational Sociology*, XVI (February, 1943), 327-328.

361 "Pisatelj Adamič prosi za podatke" [Adamic Seeks Information], *Glas naroda*, March 8, 1943, p. 2; March 9, p. 2.

362 "Your Train Is Late?" *This Week Magazine*, March 14, 1943, p. 2.

363 "Passage to the Future," *Rotarian*, LXII (March, 1943), 8-10.

364 Review of Woody Guthrie, *Bound for Glory*. "Twentieth-Century Troubador," *Saturday Review of Literature*, XXVI (April 17, 1943), 14.

365 "Meet A Hero," *This Week Magazine*, April 25, 1943, p. 2.

365a "Spoznajte junaka," *Glas naroda*, May 4, 1943, p. 2; May 5, p. 2.

366 "Who Is to Blame?" *Yugoslavia*, II (April 26, 1943), 2.

367 "Governor Harold Stassen and T-WP," "People for Postwar Service in Slovenia," "Postwar Workers for Holland," "Individual Two-Way Passengers," and "Attention: Chicagoans," *In Re: Two-Way Passage*, II (April–May, 1943), 3-4, 7.

368 "What Hitler Did to My Friends," *Saturday Evening Post*, CCXVI (July 3, 1943), 26-27, 49, 51. From *My Native Land*.

368a "Sta je Hitler uradio sa mojim prijateljima," *Slobodna Reč* (Pittsburgh), July 23, 1943, p. 2. Cyr.

368b "Sto je Hitler donio mojim prijateljima," *Novosti* (Toronto), III, 387 (1943), 4; 389 (1943), 4; 390 (1943), 4.

369 "Istra je deo Jugoslavije" [Istria Is a Part of Yugoslavia], *Slobodna Reč*, July 30, 1943, p. 1. Cyr.

369a "The Letter Sent by Louis Adamic to President Roosevelt after the Fall of the Mussolini Government," *Glas naroda*, July 30, 1943, p. 1.

369b "Pismo, ki ga je poslal znani pisatelj Louis Adamic predsedniku Rooseveltu po padcu Mussolinijeve vlade," *Glas naroda*, July 30, 1943, p. 2.

369c "A Telegram to President Roosevelt," *The Bulletin of the United Committee of South-Slavic Americans*, I (September 7, 1943), 6.

370 "Change" and "A Request to T-WP Supporters," *In Re: Two-Way Passage*, II (August–September, 1943), 1, 2-3.

371 "Bodočnost na obzorju" [The Future on the Horizon], *Glas naroda*, September 8, 1943, p. 4; September 16, p. 4.

371a *Novosti* (Toronto), III, 407 (1943), 2.

371b *Srpski glasnik*, III, 39 (1943), 2. Cyr.

372 "Can We Teach Old Europe New Tricks?" Toronto *Star Weekly*, September 11, 1943, p. 4.

372a *Predictions*, I (Fall, 1943), 84-89.

373 "Louis Adamic—Milford—New Jersey," *Nova Doba* (Cleveland), September 13, 1944, p. 6.

374 "Gen. Tito Leads Yugoslav Partisans to New Victories: Louis Adamic Lauds Peasant Fighter, Call Mikhailovitch Reputation 'Hoax,' " *PM*, September 21, 1943, p. 8.

374a "General Tito predvodi jugoslovenske partizane ka novim velikim pobedama," *Slobodna Reč* (Pittsburgh), September 24, 1943, p. 2. Cyr.

374b "Louis Adamič piše o kmečkem boritelju Titu," *Glas naroda*, September 27, 1943, p. 1; "Titova armada menda šteje 250,000 mož," September 28, p. 1.

374c "General Tito vodi jugoslavenske partizane k pobjedi. Louis Adamič veliča seljaka—borca, a Mihajlovicevu reputaciju naziva lakrdijom," *Novosti* (Toronto), III, 411 (1943), 2.

374d *Novosti* (Toronto), *III*, 421 (1943), 4.

374e "Adamič o Titu," *Napredak* (Sidney), N.S. II, 58 (1943), 3.

374f "Ko je Tito. Napisao Lj. Adamič" [Who Is Tito? By L. Adamic], *Srpski glasnik*, III, 40 (1943), 2. Cyr.

375 "Death in front of the Church," *Harper's Magazine*, CLXXXVII (September, 1943), 365-375.

376 "Milan Nedich—Will He Be Promoted from Quisling to Darlan?" *The Bulletin of the United Committee of South-Slavic Americans*, I (October 1, 1943), 1.

377 "Mikhailovitch Not a Puzzle," New York *Times*, October 15, 1943, p. 18.

377a "Mihajlovic saraduje a Nemcima, kaže L. Adamič u pismo 'Tajmsu,' " *Slobodna Reč* (Pittsburgh), October 20, 1943, p. 3. Cyr.

377b Mihajlovic nije zagonetka: 15 oktobra 1943," *Novosti* (Toronto), III, 420 (1943), 2.

378 "Russia, Britain and America: Louis Adamic Tells Why He Believes the Key to Their Problem Is Held by Yugoslav Partisans," *PM*, October 17, 1943, pp. 2-5.

379 Et al. "A Message," *The Bulletin of the United Committee of South-Slavic Americans*, I (October 20, 1943), 3-4.

379a "Izjava južnoslovenskog odbora o narodnoj vladi u Jugoslaviji. Luis Adamič" [The Statement of the United Committee of South-Slavic Americans Concerning the Government in Yugoslavia], *Slobodna Reč* (Pittsburgh), December 13, 1943, p. 1. Cyr.

379b "Zlatko Balokovic, Zarko Bunčic i dr. Pozdrav junačkim jugoslavenskim borcima iz USA. Borcima za slobodu Jugoslavije," *Novosti* (Toronto), III, 412 (1943), 1.

380 "The Yugoslav Peoples Are Through Fooling Around," *The Bulletin of the United Committee of South-Slavic Americans*, I (October 20, 1943), 1-3.

381 "Telegram Luisa Adamiča konferenciji u Moskvi" [Louis Adamic's Telegram to the Foreign Ministers' Conference in Moscow], *Slobodna Reč* (Pittsburgh), October 25, 1943, p. 1. Cyr.

381a "Traže od Moskovske konvencije da pomogne borcima u Jugoslaviji. Brzojav upucen Edenu, Hillu i Molotovu po Louis Adamiču [Asks Moscow Conference to Aid Yugoslav Fighters. Telegram Sent by Adamic to Eden, Hull, and Molotov], *Novosti* (Toronto), III, 421 (1943), 1.

382 "The Liberation Front in Yugoslavia," *Nation*, CLVII (October 30, 1943), 500-502.

383 "Talk with a Yugoslav Politician: 1942," "Of Russia and Us: Communists and Non-Communists," "The Atlantic Charter," and "It's Up to Us Americans," *War and Post-War*, II (October, 1943), 1-4.

384 "Yugoslavia," San Francisco *Chronicle*, November 10, 1943, p. 14.

384a "Adamič zagovarja Jugoslavijo," *Glas naroda*, November 24, 1943, p. 2.

384b "Mihajlovic agent reakcije" [Mikhailovitch Agent of Reactionaries], *Slobodna Reč* (Pittsburgh), November 24, 1943, p. 2. Cyr.

385 Review of Hans Natonek, *In Search of Myself*. "An Individualist-at-Large," *Saturday Review of Literature*, XXVI (November 13, 1943), 5.

386 "Saveznici moraju da odbace Mihajlovica i četnik. Radio govor Luisa Adamiča" [The Allies Must Reject Mikhailovitch and the Chetniks: Louis Adamic's Radio Speech], *Slobodna Reč* (Pittsburgh), November 17, 1943, p. 2. Cyr.

386a "Prijetnja bez osnove," *Novosti* (Toronto), III, 434 (1943), 2.

387 "Govor pisatelja Louisa Adamiča na shodu SANS—a v Clevelandu, Ohio" [Louis Adamic's Speech at the Conference of SANS in Cleveland, Ohio], *Glas naroda*, November 23, 1943, p. 4; November 24, p. 3; November 26, p. 3.

388 Et al. "The Battle for the Balkans: Round Table No. 20," *Free World*, VI (November, 1943), 424-439.

389 "Louis Adamic Says: Tito Wins Big Powers' Support," *PM*, December 12, 1943, p. 7.

390 "Slovenima Amerike. Iz govora L. Adamiča preko radia, Cikago, 9 decembra" [To the Slavs of America. L. Adamic's Radio Speech, Chicago, December 9], *Slobodna Reč* (Pittsburgh), December 15, 1943, p. 3. Cyr.

390a "Adamičev govor preko Kanadian Broadcasting System" [Adamic's Speech over the Canadian Broadcasting System], *Novosti* (Toronto), III, 431 (1943), 1.

390b "Louis Adamič Speaks over Canadian Broadcasting Co.," *Novosti* (Toronto), III, 432 (1943), 4.

391 "Izčrpek iz govora Louisa Adamica v Carnegie Hall" [Excerpt from Louis Adamic's Carnegie Hall Speech], *Glas naroda*, December 27, 1943, p. 2.

392 Et al. "Freedom from Fear: A Panel Discussion from the Third Free World Congress," *Free World*, VI (December, 1943), 514-523.

392a "La Liberacion del Temor," *Mundo Libre*, III (February, 1944), 24-32.

393 "L. Adamič o situaciji u Jugoslaviji" [Louis Adamic about the Situation in Yugoslavia], *Napredak* (Sidney), N.S. I, 18 (1943), 2; "Adamič o Jugoslaviji" [Adamic about Yugoslavia], 21 (1943), 2. From *Inside Yugoslavia.*

394 "Protest radi podržavanja fašističkih generala. Zrtve jugoslovenskog naroda traže da njegova prava budu poštivana, a fašistički zločinci kažnjeni" [A Protest Against

Support of Fascist Generals. Yugoslav Victims Ask That Their Rights Be Respected and the Fascist Criminals Be Punished (to Gen. D. D. Eisenhower)], *Novosti* (Toronto), III, 425 (1943), 1.

395 "Sto su ciljevi ujedinjenog Odbora američkih Hrvata, Srba i Slovenaca. Od Louis Adamiča" [What Are the Goals of the United Committee of South-Slavic Americans—from Louis Adamic], *Novosti* (Toronto), III, 386 (1943), 2.

396 "U vezi sa najnovijim dogadajima u Jugoslaviji. New York, 6. dec." [In View of the Latest Events in Yugoslavia], *Novosti* (Toronto), III, 444 (1943), 2.

397 "A National Agency Must Have Authority," *Common Ground*, IV (Winter, 1944), 17-18.

398 "Jačajmo jedinstvo Slovena u borbi protiv reakcije" [Let's Strengthen the Unity of Slavs in the Fight against Reaction], *Slobodna Reč* (Pittsburgh), January 26, 1944, p. 2. Cyr. Telegram to the All Slav Congress.

399 "Dogadaji u Jugoslaviji su od velike važnosti za Sjedinjene Države: Milford, Nju Jersi, januara 1944" [Events in Yugoslavia Are of Great Importance for the United States: Milford, New Jersey, January, 1944], *Slobodna Reč* (Pittsburgh), January 31, 1944, p. 2. Cyr.

400 "Reply," *War and Post-War*, III (January–February, 1944), 1-6.

401 "Traže se osobe za rad u Jugoslaviji: Milford, Nju Jerzi" [People Sought for Work in Yugoslavia], *Slobodna Reč* (Pittsburgh), March 3, 1944, p. 1. Cyr.

401a "Government Appeals for Trained People," *Slobodna Reč* (Pittsburgh), March 6, 1944, p. 4.

402 "A Letter," *The Bulletin of the United Committee of South-Slavic Americans*, II (March 10, 1944), 7.

402a "Jugoslavensko pitanje je demokratsko pitanje. Pismo Louis Adamiča američkom listu 'Pittsburgh press,' " *Napredak* (Sidney), N.S. II, 81 (1944), 3.

403 "Istorija če smatra Tita jednim od najvecih voda u ovom svetskom ratu. Govor Luisa Adamica na banketu književnika u Njujorku 7 marta 1944 godine" [History Will Record Tito As One of the Greatest Leaders of the War. Louis Adamic's Speech at the Book and Author Luncheon in New York, March 7, 1944], *Slobodna Reč* (Pittsburgh), March 10, 1944, p. 2. Cyr.

403a "History Will Record Tito As One of the Greatest Heroes of This War, Said Louis Adamic at a Banquet in New York," *Slobodna Reč* (Pittsburgh), March 13, 1944, p. 4.

403b "Kongresni zapisnik objavljuje Adamičev govor," *Slobodna Reč* (Pittsburgh), June 17, 1944, p. 3. Cyr.

404 "Adamic Suggests Tito Is Factor," New York *Times*, March 14, 1944, p. 36.

405 "Yugoslavia: March 27, 1941—March 27, 1944," *The Bulletin of the United Committee of South-Slavic Americans*, II (March 17, 1944), 1-3.

406 "A Letter from Louis Adamic," *The Hammond Times* (Indiana), March 29, 1944, p. 22.

407 "Yugoslavia, Tito and The 'Partisans,' " *Dalhousie Review*, XXIV (April, 1944), 1-10.

408 Review of Laird Archer, *Balkan Journal: An Unofficial Observer in Greece*. "They Could Not Conquer," New York *Herald Tribune*, May 7, 1944, Sec. VI, p. 12.

409 "A Note in Connection with Father Orlemanski," *War and Post-War*, III (May–June, 1944), 1-2.

410 "Yugoslavia and the Big United Nations, *Slavonic and East European Review*, XXII (May, 1944) (American Series, III, I), 1-15.

411 "Adamic Praises M. J. Bogdanovich," San Pedro *News-Pilot*, June 27, 1944, p. 3.

411a "Umro je u radu za narod" [He Died Working for the Nation], *Slobodna Reč* (Pittsburgh), June 29, 1944, p. 3. Cyr.

412 "An Editorial Written by an Immigrant for Immigrants and Their Descendants—In Other Words, for Americans," *Woman's Day* (July, 1944), 21. The introduction to the *Woman's Day* "They Believed in Liberty" series. Each article in the series was illustrated by a painting of a person typical of the nationality being discussed. At a cost of ten cents for each set, *Woman's Day* offered its readers a reprint of the text on a sheet twelve and one half by sixteen and one half inches and a reproduction of the painting on a sheet ten by thirteen inches. The name of the artist commissioned for each article appears in parentheses at the end of the entry for items in the series. Following the introductory "Editorial" in this same July issue was the first article in the series—"They Believed in Liberty: Americans from Greece," 22-23, 47, 52 (Henry Varnum Poor).

413 "The European War's End" and "Two-Way Passage Idea at Work," *War and Post-War*, III (July–August, 1944), 1, 6.

414 "Peace as a World Race Problem," *The University of Chicago Round Table*, No. 335 (August 20, 1944), 1-20. Adamic's participation in a radio discussion, especially concerning the colored peoples.

415 "They Believed in Liberty: Americans from Poland," *Woman's Day* (August, 1944), 24-25, 68-72 (Ernest Fiene). *See above* no. 412.

416 Et al. "Statement," *New Masses*, LII (September 5, 1944), 24. Adamic was one of the signatories of this statement by the Independent Voters' Committee of Arts and Sciences for Roosevelt.

417 "Italians and Germans," *War and Post-War*, III (September–October, 1944), 3.

417a "Italijani in Nemci," *Glas naroda*, October 9, 1944, p. 2.

418 Review of Fred L. Holmes, *Old World Wisconsin: Around Europe in the Badger State*. *Wisconsin Magazine of History*, XXVIII (September, 1944), 87-89.

419 "They Believed in Liberty: Americans from Ireland," *Woman's Day* (September, 1944), 24-25, 52, 56 (Marion Greenwood). *See above* no. 412.

420 "Commends Editorials," Toronto *Daily Star*, October 14, 1944, p. 10.

421 "Adamič apelira za pomoč Jugoslaviji" [Adamic Appeals for Aid for Yugoslavia], *Glas naroda*, October 27, 1944, p. 2.

421a "U oslobodenu Jugoslaviju dolazi zima i Božic! Jedan apel Luisa Adamiča" [To Liberated Yugoslavia Come Winter and Christmas! An Appeal from Louis Adamic], *Slobodna Reč* (Pittsburgh), October 28, 1944, p. 3. Cyr.

422 "They Believed in Liberty: Americans from Italy," *Woman's Day* (October, 1944), 40-41, 79-85 (Alexander Brook). *See above* no. 412.

422a *Sons of Italy Magazine*, XVII (December, 1944), 8-10.

423 "A Letter to Governor Lehman," *The Bulletin of the United Committee of South-Slavic Americans*, II (November, 1944), 8.

424 "Is the U.S.A. in Danger of Becoming a Catholic State?" *War and Post-War*, III (November-December, 1944), 5-8.

425 "They Believed in Liberty: Americans from Norway," *Woman's Day* (November, 1944), 42-43, 54, 58, 60 (William Langdon Kihn). *See above* no. 412.

426 "Why Our People Hate the Nazis," *Read*, XVI (November, 1944), 27-32. From *My Native Land*.

427 "Yugoslavia: What Her Struggle Means to America," *The Christian Register: Unitarian*, CXXIII (November, 1944), 389-390.

428 "Louis Adamic Greets 10th Anniversary of 'Slobodna Reč,' " *Slobodna Reč* (Pittsburgh), December 12, 1944, p. 4.

429 "They Believed in Liberty: Americans from France," *Woman's Day* (December, 1944), 40-41, 73-76 (Umberto Romano). *See above* no. 412.

430 "Nije istina. New York, 1 marča" [It Is Not True: New York, March 1], *Novosti* (Toronto), IV, 475 (1944), 1.

431 "Zlatko Balokovic i Strahinja Maletic. Beograd osloboden . . ." [Zlatko Balokovic and Strahinja Maletic: Belgrade Freed . . .], *Novosti* (Toronto), IV 575 (1944), 2.

432 "American Committee for Yugoslav Relief," *Glas naroda*, January 22, 1945, p. 2.

433 "Guns for Tito," *The Bulletin of the United Committee of South-Slavic Americans*, III (January–February, 1945), 9.

434 "Notes for Historians of the Yugoslav Revolution," "Inside Greece," and "The 'Polish Problem,' " *Today & Tomorrow*, I (January–February, 1945), 4, 5-6.

435 "Tito Simply Had to Win in Yugoslavia," *Today & Tomorrow*, I (January–February, 1945), 1-4.

435a "Zakaj je Tito moral zmagati. Piše Louis Adamič v publikaciji 'Today and Tomorrow,' " *Glas naroda*, February 14, 1945, p. 2; February 15, p. 2; February 16, p. 3.

436 "They Believed in Liberty: Americans from Yugoslavia," *Woman's Day* (January, 1945), 24-25, 50, 57-60 (Jerry Farnsworth). *See above* no. 412.

436a Editors of *Slobodna Reč*, *Serbian National Calendar* (Pittsburgh: Slobodna Reč, 1945), pp. 61-65. Cyr.

437 "The Name 'T & T,' " *T & T*, I (March–April, 1945), 8.

438 "They Believed in Liberty: Americans from Russia," *Woman's Day* (March, 1945), 40-41, 82-90 (Joseph Hirsch). *See above* no. 412.

439 "Trieste: A Vital Challenge to the Big 3: Are British Trying to Weaken Tito—And Where Do We Come In?" *PM*, May 20, 1945, p. 10.

440 "Neglected Americana," *The Book Find News*, II (May, 1945), 7.

441 "We and the Soviet Union, and World War III" and "Letter to a Friend—Preface to A Nation of Nations," *T & T: Trends and Tides,* I (May–July, 1945), 1, 9-13.

442 "Midsummer Notes," " 'Anglo-American' Diplomats and Tito," and "Figures and Flashes in the American Maze: Excerpts from Louis Adamic's forthcoming book *A Nation of Nations,*" *T & T: Trends and Tides,* I (August–September, 1945), 1-2, 2-3, 6-8.

443 "They Believed in Liberty: Americans from Sweden," *Woman's Day* (August, 1945), 24-25, 48, 50-51, 56-57 (Esther Williams). *See above* no. 412.

444 Et al. "A Letter to President Truman," "Alfred Korzybski and General Semantics," and "The Story of Gus Korach," *T & T: Trends and Tides,* I (October, 1945), 1-2, 6-8.

445 Cable to Ernest Bevin and "America Is American: Address by Louis Adamic, Children's Book Council Luncheon, Hotel Astor, New York, November 12," *T & T: Trends and Tides,* I (November–December, 1945), 4, 9-12.

446 "On November 2 Louis Adamic Replied," *The Bulletin of the United Committee of South-Slavic Americans,* III (December, 1945), 7-9.

447 "Who Represents the U.S. in Southeastern Europe?" and "New Revision of 'Dynamite,' " *T & T: Trends and Tides,* II (January–February, 1946), 1-3, 5.

448 "They Believed in Liberty: Americans from Holland," *Woman's Day* (February, 1946), 28-29, 90-92, 94-98 (Waldo Peirce). *See above* no. 412.

449 "Clanging with a Loud and Snarling Note" and "Mutterings of a Missouri Mule," *T & T: Trends and Tides*, II (March–May, 1946), 1-2, 6.

450 "There Are Whites and Whites," *Negro Digest*, IV (March, 1946), 47-50.

451 "Words to Live By: Louis Adamic," *This Week Magazine*, May 19, 1946, p. 2.

451a "A Nation of Nations," William I. Nichols, ed., *Words to Live By: A Little Treasury of Inspiration and Wisdom Selected and Interpreted by Eighty-four Eminent Men and Women* (New York: Simon and Schuster, 1948), pp. 100-101.

452 "Telegram," *The Bulletin of the United Committee of South-Slavic Americans*, IV (May, 1946), 6.

453 "Adamic's Letter to Sec'y Byrnes on Trieste Issue," *Prosveta*, June 19, 1946, pp. 6, 8.

454 "Rules for Reducing the United States as a Great Power" and "My Reply (April 29)," *T & T: Trends & Tides*, II (June–July, 1946), 1-2, 3-4.

455 "Dinner at the White House," *T & T: Trends & Tides*, II (August–September, 1946), 5-8.

456 "The Mikhailovich Case," *T & T: Trends & Tides*, II (August–September, 1946), 3-4.

456a "The Case of Drazha Mikhailovich," *The Bulletin of the United Committee of South-Slavic Americans*, IV (September, 1946), 22-23.

457 "Adamic Charges Allies Shelter Yugo Quislings," *PM*, September 2, 1946, pp. 1, 8-9.

458 "Escuela Agricola Panamerica," *Woman's Day* (September, 1946), 30-31, 66-70.

459 "The Truth about the American-Yugoslav Crisis," *The Bulletin of the United Committee of South-Slavic Americans*, IV (September, 1946), 1-4.

460 "The Little Man in the White House," "Notes on American-Yugoslav Relations," and "Yugoslavia and German Defeat," *T & T: Trends & Tides*, II (October–December, 1946), 1-9, 11-12, 13-14.

461 "Don't Let Your Faith in America Waver," *The Bulletin of the United Committee of South-Slavic Americans*, IV (December, 1946), 28.

462 "The Contest: An Address Given by Louis Adamic in the First Unitarian Church of Essex County, Orange, N. J., on Jan. 26," "Dynamite," and "Letter to Shaemas O'Sheel, dated Jan. 25," *T & T: Trends & Tides*, III (January–March, 1947), 1-4, 7, 13.

463 "Tolerance Is Not Enough," *T & T: Trends & Tides*, III (January–March, 1947), 14-15.

463a *Progressive World*, II (May, 1948), 141-144.

464 "Should We Raise Immigration Quotas?" *WGN (Northwestern University) on the Air: The Reviewing Stand*, VIII (February 23, 1947), 3. Adamic's opening of the program.

465 "Of Greece and Oil . . . Of Truman and Toynbee," *T & T: Trends & Tides*, III (April–June, 1947), 1-9.

465a "Truman's Ties to Oil Men Date Back," Valley City *Times-Record* (North Dakota), May 26, 1947, pp. 4, 6.

465b "Herbert Hoover, Jr., Has Oil Connections," Valley City *Times-Record* (North Dakota), May 28, 1947, p. 6.

466 "Murder in Peoria," *T & T: Trends & Tides*, III (April–June, 1947), 19-21.

466a *Labor Review*, XXII (August 29, 1947), 11-13.

467 "The Enormous Distortion: An Address by Louis Adamic, Delivered at a Rally Sponsored by the Chicago Council of American-Soviet Friendship on March 9. . . ," *T & T: Trends & Tides*, III (April–June, 1947), 11-14.

468 "Will American Labor, Too, Learn Only the Hard Way?" "Business or War—Alternatives in American-Soviet Affairs," and "The Peoples of America Series," *T & T: Trends & Tides*, III (July–September, 1947), 1-2, 5-8, 12.

469 "Politics in the Pentagon and World War III: The Significant Case of General H. C. Holdridge. . . ," "On Being a Crackpot," "A Man and His Garters," "My Friend 'Cvyetko,' " and "The Problem of Publishing T & T," *T & T: Trends & Tides*, III (October–December, 1947), 1, 8-9, 15, 17, 24.

470 "Večerja v beli hiši" [Dinner at the White House], *Novi Svet* (Ljubljana), II (1947), 290-302. Translated by Mira Puc. From *Dinner at the White House.*

470a "Vecera u bijeloj kuci," *Ilustrirani Vjesnik*, April 24, 1948, pp. 6-7.

471 " 'All Men Are Created Equal'—Do We Mean It or Don't We?" *T & T: Trends & Tides*, IV (January–March, 1948), 1-8.

472 "Headlines and History, Hysteria and Hypocrisy" and "The Wrap and Woof of America," *T & T: Trends & Tides*, IV (April–June, 1948), 4-8, 23, 30.

473 "Adamic Blasts Catholicism; Claims Vatican Wants War," *The Cement News* (Northampton, Pennsylvania), May 13, 1948, pp. 1, 4.

474 "Hull Quoted by Adamic as Basis for Pro-Red Stand," *The Cement News* (Northampton, Pennsylvania), May 27, 1948, pp. 1, 12.

475 "One's Own Dwelling," *The Perfect Home*, n.v. (June, 1948), 3.

476 "History as a Record and a Process," *Common Ground*, VIII (Summer, 1948), 20-23.

476a "Two Ways of Seeing Our History," Ivan E. Taylor and J. Saunders Redding, eds., *Reading for Writing* (New York: Ronald Press, 1952), pp. 291-301.

477 "Tito vs. Cominform: A Question of Manners," New York *Star*, July 11, 1948, p. 16.

477a "Tito-Stalin Rift 'The Bunk,' " New Orleans *Item*, July 31, 1948.

477b "Cominform and Yugoslavia," *T & T: Trends & Tides*, IV (July–September, 1948), 8.

478 "Needed: Friendly Reciprocity" and "Now, What about Communism?" *T & T: Trends & Tides*, IV (July–September, 1948), 11-12, 13.

479 With R. V. Cassill, "Henry Wallace Is 'In It'—He's Already Won," *T & T: Trends & Tides*, IV (July–September, 1948), 1-4.

480 "We Need One Another," *Soviet Russia Today*, XVII (July, 1948), 11, 27.

[*** On August 7, 1948, Adamic wrote to a friend: "I did not write anything about the Convention [of the Progressive Party] itself—except a little piece on one aspect of it for the new weekly paper, The National Gazette, which is trying to get started. I enclose a clipping of this piece." Adamic was referring to the Preview Issue of the weekly which became *The National Guardian: The Progressive Newsweekly*, which was published by J. W. Gitt, editor and publisher of the York *Gazette and Daily* (Pennsylvania). The official first issue of *The National Guardian* (vol. I, no. 1, October 18, 1948) verifies the Preview Issue but notes that Gitt had withdrawn as publisher. Item no. 1112 below quotes Louis Adamic in the Preview Issue of the Guardian, August 1, 1948; and the quotation may be the whole of the "little piece on one aspect" to which Adamic referred. No copy of the rare Preview Issue has been examined; and it is thus impossible here to verify the exact title of the Preview Issue and the title, if any, and the page of the article.]

481 "Adamic Replies to 'Neighborly' Critic: Reasserts 'Smear' Is Anti-Wallace Move," *Delaware Valley News* (Frenchtown, New Jersey), August 20, 1948, p. 3.

482 "Tolerance Is Bad," *McCall's*, LXXV (August, 1948), 2, 122.

482a "Tolerance Is Bad for America," *Negro Digest*, VI (October, 1948), 19-23.

483 "Adamic Sees 'The American Way of Life' Threatened by Greed," *Delaware Valley News* (Frenchtown, New Jersey), September 3, 1948, p. 3.

484 "Adamic Concludes Kinnaird Debate by Interpreting World's History," *Delaware Valley News* (Frenchtown, New Jersey), September 17, 1948, p. 3.

484a "Adamic Concludes Debate by Interpreting History," *Hunterdon County Democrat* (Flemington, New Jersey), September 23, 1948, p. 19.

485 "Do You Want *T & T* to Continue in 1949?" "How to Resist," "The Issue: The American Way," and "On Tolerance," *T & T: Trends & Tides*, IV (October–December, 1948), 17, 18, 19-22, 27-29.

486 "Tolerance—Counterfeit of Intolerance," *Congress Weekly: A Review of Jewish Interests*, XVI (January 17, 1949), 8-10.

487 "Back from Eight Months in Europe—Six in Yugoslavia," *T & T: Trends & Tides*, V (Mid-Autumn, 1949), 1-8.

487a "Zopet doma po osmih mesecih v Europe in 6 mesecih v Jugoslaviji," Izgradnja Socijalističkog Društa, *Resnica o Jugoslaviji prodira v svet* (Beograd: Slovenskega poročevalca, 1950).

488 "Yugoslavia: A Strong People with Exceptional Leadership," *Yugoslav Fortnightly*, November 2, 1949, p. 4.

489 "Of Tito and Heresy," "Revolution Comes to My Native Slovenia," "Insights into the Cominform Split: Early 1949," and "Civil Rights Through Demagogy," *T & T: Trends & Tides*, VI (Early Spring, 1950), 1, 4-12 and 28-29, 13-16, 25.

490 " 'So Strange . . . So Very Strange—,' " "This *T & T* and the New Book," "Tito—A Looming Figure," "The Poet in His Grave . . . And the Trouble with Giants," and "Tito Between the 'Giants,' " *T & T: Trends & Tides*, VI (Mid-Spring, 1950), 1, 2, 3-8, 9-15, 15-16.

491 "V Zagrebu leta 1932" [Zagreb: 1932], *Slovenski poročevalec*, XII, 210 (1951). From *The Native's Return.*

492 Posthumous. "Confessions of a 33rd Degree Subversive," *Nation*, CLXXIV (June 28, 1952), 637. From the unpublished portion of *The Eagle and the Roots.*

493 "Iz življenja maršala Tita" [From the Life of Marshal Tito], *Obzornik*, VII, 5 (1952), 257-266. From *The Eagle and the Roots.*

493a "O življenju maršala Tita," *Ljubljanski dnevnik*, II, 116 (1952); 135 (1952).

494 "Prva bomba" [The First Bomb], *Slovenski poročevalec*, XIII, 12 (1952). Translated by Ivan Crnagoj. From *Dynamite.*

495 "Razgovori z maršalom Titom" [Talks with Marshal Tito], *Primorski dnevnik* (Trst), VIII, 124 (1952), 2120; 129 (1952), 2125; 147 (1952), 2143. From *The Eagle and the Roots.*

496 "Iz pisma prijatelju v Kaliforniji" [From a Letter to a Friend in California: slightly revised], *Naša sodobnost* (Ljubljana), I, 10 (1953), 883-896. Translated by Mira Mihelic. From *The Eagle and the Roots.*

497 "John Bull osebno" [John Bull in Person], *Naši razgledi* (Ljubljana), III, 11 (1954), 12-13. Translated by H[erbert] G[rün]. From *Dinner at the White House.*

498 "Medeni Janez [Honey John], *Slovenski Jadran* (Koper), III, 31 (1954), 7. From *My America.*

499 "Večerja v Beli hiši" [Dinner at the White House], *Zbornik Občine Grosuplje: Gospodarska, Kulturna in Zgodovinska Kronika* (Grosuplje), I (1969), 121-124. Translated by Zarja Perovšek. From *Dinner at the White House.*

II. Pamphlets and Books

500 Anon. *Yugoslav Proverbs*. Ten Cent Pocket Series No. 380. Girard, Kansas: Haldeman-Julius, 1923.

500a *Yugoslav Proverbs*. Little Blue Book No. 380. Girard, Kansas: Haldeman-Julius, 1923. The "Ten Cent Pocket Series" edition with a new "Little Blue Book" cover (ca. 1924) bearing under the title the notation "Compiled by Louis Adamic."

501 Trans. *Yerney's Justice*, by Ivan Cankar. New York: Vanguard Press, 1926.

502 With Edward Campbell, Robert B. Mason, and Mike Schindler. *The Truth About Aimee Semple McPherson*. Big Blue Book No. 28. Girard, Kansas: Haldeman-Julius, 1926. Contains Adamic's "Aimee McPherson's Great Faith Factory," pp. 5-14; "The Mystery of Aimee Semple McPherson," pp. 25-30; "Aimee Semple McPherson's Hoax of the Century," pp. 31-36; "Aimee Semple McPherson's Fight with Satan," pp. 39-48; and "Was Aimee McPherson's 'Shack' in The Grove of Aphrodite?" p. 49-64.

503 Et al. *Facts You Should Know About California*. Little Blue Book No. 752. Girard, Kansas: Haldeman-Julius, 1928. Contains Adamic's "The Bright Side of Los Angeles," pp. 3-19; and "Paganism in Los Angeles," pp. 19-27.

504 *The Word of Satan in the Bible: Christians Rightly Regard Ecclesiastes Suspiciously.* Little Blue Book No. 1307. Girard, Kansas: Haldeman-Julius, 1928. Contains Adamic's "The Word of Satan in the Bible," pp. 3-27; and essays by Le Roy A. Born, T. Swann Harding, and Morrow Mayo.

505 *Robinson Jeffers: A Portrait.* University of Washington Chapbooks No. 27. Seattle: University of Washington Book Store, 1929.

506 *Dynamite: The Story of Class Violence in America.* New York: Viking, 1931.

506a *Dynamite: The Story of Class Violence in America.* London: Jonathan Cape, 1931. With an introduction by S. K. Ratcliffe.

506b *Dinamit: povijest klasnog nasilja u Americi.* Translated by Dr. Branko Kojic. Zagreb: "Binoza," 1933.

507 *Laughing in the Jungle: The Autobiography of an Immigrant in America.* New York and London: Harper, 1932.

507a *Smeh v džungli: avtobiografija ameriškega priseljenca.* Translated by Stanko Leben. Ljubljana: Tiskovna zadruga, 1933.

507b *Smijeh u džungli: autobiografija jednog američkog useljenika.* Translated by Dr. Branko Kojic. Zagreb: "Binoza," 1933.

507b* Sarajevo: Seljačka Knjiga, 1952. The "Binoza" edition reprinted in Cyrillic.

507c *Laughing in the Jungle: The Autobiography of an Immigrant in America.* No. AMO3 in The American Immigration Collection: Series I. New York: Arno Press and The New York Times, 1969.

508 *Kriza v Ameriki* [Crisis in America]. Translated by Anton Debeljak. Ljubljana: Tiskovna zadruga, 1932. Published articles, newly edited.

509 *Home Again from America: An Immigrant Revists His Native Land.* New York: "Reprinted from Harper's Magazine, October, 1932," [1932].

510 *The Native's Return: An American Immigrant Visits Yugoslavia and Discovers His Old Country.* New York and London: Harper, 1934. Book-of-the-Month Club selection for February, 1934. By September 1, 1938, Adamic had advised Harper and Bros. "to cut out of the plates everything after line 24 on page 358. . . . entire pages 359-370, which includes the index. The book, thus, ends with the sentence: 'I had an enormous lump in my throat.' " These deletions were effected in the 19th edition, marked K-N for October, 1938 (a printing of October 18). The four unnumbered pages beginning "Critical Comment on 'Laughing in the Jungle' by Louis Adamic" which had followed p. 370 now followed the 358th page, which was also now left unnumbered. All subsequent editions in English by all publishers end in this manner.

510a *The Native's Return: An American Immigrant Visits Yugoslavia and Discovers His Old Country.* London: Victor Gollancz, 1934.

510b *Hemkomsten: En Emigrant Upptäcker Sitt Gamla Fosterland.* Translated by Valdemar Georg Langlet. Stockholm: Bokförlaget Natur Och Kultur, 1934.

510c *The Native's Return: An American Immigrant Visits Yugoslavia and Discovers His Old Country.* Harper's Modern Classics edition. New York and London: Harper, 1937. Lacks illustrations.

510d *The Native's Return: An Autobiography by Louis Adamic.* Armed Services Edition B-54. New York: Council on Books in Wartime, Incorporated, [1944]. Edition follows Adamic's 1938 instructions but omits "Critical Comment. . . ." Lacks illustrations.

510e *Vrnitev v rodni Kraj.* Translated by Mira Mihelič. Ljubljana: Cankarjeva založba, 1962.

511 Trans. *Struggle*, by "a young Communist" [Edvard Kardelj]. Los Angeles: Arthur Whipple, 1934. Preface by Adamic.

511a With Georgi Dimitrov and Pierre Van Passen. *George Dimitroff, Pierre Van Passen* [,] *Louis Adamic on the Bloody Fascist Terror in the Balkans.* Detroit: The Macedonian People's League of America, [ca. 1934]. "Torture in Belgrade," pp. 5-15, is the translation portion of *Struggle.*

511b *Struggle.* New York: Tomorrow Publishers, 1935.

511c *Boj.* Translated by Jože Stabej. Ljubljana: Državna založba Slovenije, 1969. Introduction by Ivan Bratko.

512 *Dynamite: The Story of Class Violence in America.* Revised Edition. New York: Viking, 1934. Substantially changed from 1931 edition following p. 402.

512a *Dynamite: The Story of Class Violence in America.* Revised Edition. Gloucester, Massachusetts: Peter Smith, 1960. Also another reprinting by Peter Smith in 1963.

512b *Dynamite: The Story of Class Violence in America.* Revised Edition. Cherry Pie Series. New York and London: Chelsea House Publishers, [1969]. Distributed as Chelsea House/Vintage No. V-602.

513 *Grandsons: A Story of American Lives.* New York and London: Harper, 1935.

513a *Grandsons: A Story of American Lives.* London: Victor Gollancz, 1935.

513b *Vnuki: zgodba iz ameriških usod.* Translated by Mira Mihelič. Ljubljana: Cankarjeva založba, 1951.

514 *Lucas, King of the Balucas.* Los Angeles: Arthur Whipple, 1935. Limited to 350 copies.

515 *Thirty Million New Americans.* New York: Service Bureau for Education in Human Relations, 1935. Reprinted from *Harper's Magazine.*

516 *Cradle of Life: The Story of One Man's Beginnings.* New York and London: Harper, 1936.

516a *Cradle of Life: The Story of One Man's Beginnings.* London: Victor Gollancz, 1937.

517 *The House in Antigua: A Restoration.* New York and London: Harper, 1937.

517a *The House in Antigua: A Restoration.* London: Victor Gollancz, 1938.

518 *My America: 1928–1938.* New York and London: Harper, 1938.

518a *My America: 1928–1938.* London: Hamish Hamilton, 1938.

519 *Walter Locke of Dayton: A Free Editor.* [Probably Dayton, Ohio: *Daily News*, ca. 1939.] "Excerpt Reprinted from the Popular Book 'My America' by Louis Adamic."

520 *America and the Refugees.* Public Affairs Pamphlets No. 29. New York: Public Affairs Committee, Inc., February, 1939. Revised edition, October, 1939. Third revised edition, May 1940.

521 *From Many Lands.* New York and London: Harper, 1940. No. 1 of the Nation of Nations series. Second and subsequent editions bear the copyright date "1939, 1940."

521a *Crisol de razas: Historia de los hombres de muchas tierras que hicieron la grandeza de estados unidos.* Translated by León Mirlas. Bibloteca de Obras Famosas, Volumen 88. Buenos Aires: Editorial Claridad, 1942.

522 *Plymouth Rock and Ellis Island.* New York: Common Council for American Unity, 1940. Summary of a lecture given in various forms between October, 1939, and March, 1940.

523 *This Crisis Is an Opportunity.* New York: Common Council for American Unity, 1940.

524 *On Unity and Uniformity.* Cleveland: The Cleveland Council for American Unity, 1941.

525 *Two-Way Passage.* New York and London: Harper, 1941. No. 2 of the Nation of Nations series. The sixth edition (a printing of November 20, 1942) and all subsequent editions differ following p. 298.

526 *The Passage Back.* Laguna Beach, California: Ray Marsh Fox, 1942. A revised form of the final chapter of the 6th and subsequent editions of *Two-Way Passage.*

527 Et al. *Sincerely Yours: A Correspondence*. New York: "Reprinted from *Contemporary Jewish Record*, October, 1942," [1942].

528 *Inside Yugoslavia*. Ridgefield, Connecticut: Acorn Press, 1942. Limited edition as a supplement to the journal *Yugoslavia*, Vol. 1, December 15, 1942.

529 *What's Your Name?* New York and London: Harper, 1942. No. 3 of the Nation of Nations series.

530 *My Native Land*. New York and London: Harper, 1943.

530a *My Native Land*. New York: Book Find Club, 1943.

531 Trans. *Testament of a Dying Partisan*. [Probably New York: United Committee of South Slavic-Americans, ca. 1943.] Five sides of a six fold paper. On p. 477 of *My Native Land*, Adamic noted: "There are several versions of this letter. . . . One appeared in a London paper called *The People* early in '43. Stoyan Pribichevich . . . got hold of another and sent it to *Time*, which published it in February '43. The Pribichevich version was reprinted in *Readers Digest* and broadcast over 'The March of Time' program." Pribichevich, a *Time* Staff Correspondent writing under the name P. B. Stoyan, published the letter as "Such Is Your Heritage," *Time Magazine*, January 25, 1943, p. 33.

531a *Oporuka umiruceg partizana*. New York: United Committee of South-Slavic Americans, 1943.

532 *Wanted: An Approach to the Postwar Problem*. Central and Eastern Planning Board, New York. Pamphlet series No. 4. New York: "New Europe," 1943.

533 Et al. *The Battle for the Balkans*. New York: United Committee of South-Slavic Americans, 1943. Reprinted from *Free World*.

534 With George F. Addes. *Foreign-Born Americans and the War*. New York: American Committee for Protection of the Foreign Born, 1943. Contains Adamic's "The Foreign Born Unite for Victory," a speech delivered at the tenth anniversary National Conference of the American Committee . . . Born, pp. 3-13.

535 *1944 . . . Crucial Year: The Need of "Dynamic" Unity in the Immigrant Groups*. New York: United Committee of South-Slavic Americans, 1944. Contains two addresses by Adamic: "For *Dynamic* Unity in the Immigrant Groups," an altered title for his same speech at the tenth anniversary National Conference of the American Committee . . . Born (*see above* no. 534); and "1944 . . . Crucial Year," excerpts from his speech at the American Slav Congress Rally in Detroit, December 12, 1943.

536 Ed., and with Winston Churchill, Sergeant Walter Bernstein, Frank Gervasi, and Stoyan Pribichevich. *Marshal Tito and His Gallant Bands*. New York: United Committee of South-Slavic Americans, 1944. Contains Adamic's "A Study in Courage," pp. 9-10.

537 Ed. Sulzberger, C. L. *Tito's Yugoslav Partisan Movement*. New York: United Committee of South-Slavic Americans, 1944. Preface by Adamic, p. 3.

538 Ed. Tito, J. B., Dr. Josip Smodlaka, and Fran Barbalich. *Yugoslavia and Italy*. New York: United Committee of South-Slavic Americans, 1944. Foreword by Adamic, p. 3.

539 *The Yugoslav Problem Is Also an American Problem: Louis Adamic Answers the Pittsburgh Press*. New York: United Committee of South-Slavic Americans, 1944.

540 *A Nation of Nations*. New York and London: Harper, 1945. No. 4 of the Nation of Nations series.

541 *Letter to an Old-Line American of Anglo-Saxon Stock*. Milford, New Jersey: "Reprinted, in abbreviated form, from *A Nation of Nations*," [1945].

542 Ed. *Liberation. Death to Fascism! Liberty to the People! Picture Story of the Yugoslav People's Epic Struggle Against the Enemy—To Win Unity and a Decent Future, 1941–1945*. New York: United Committee of South-Slavic Americans, 1945.

543 *America and Trieste: God and the Russians: A Letter to the Honorable James F. Byrnes, Secretary of State*. New York: United Committee of South-Slavic Americans, 1946.

544 *Dinner at the White House*. New York and London: Harper, 1946. In November of 1946, the plates for pp. 151-152 were altered to delete the footnote thereon; and the printing of November 13, 1946, marked M-V, omits the footnote. In some first editions the footnote was cut from the bottom of the page before distribution.

544a *Večere v Bílém domě*. Translated by Vladimír V. Bernášek. Praha: Mlada-Fronta, 1947.

545 Ed. *The Peoples of America Series*. Philadelphia: Lippincott, 1947–1950. Although General Editor for nine of the series, Adamic published but these three prefaces:

545a "The Peoples of America Series," in Arnold Mulder, *Americans from Holland* (1947), pp. 5-8.

545b "The Warp and Woof of America," in Emil Lengyel, *Americans from Hungary* (1948), pp. 7-8.

545c "On Tolerance," in Bradford Smith, *Americans from Japan* (1948), pp. vii-xii.

545d The other volumes in the series are Gerald W. Johnson, *Our English Heritage*, 1949; D'Arcy McNickle, *They Came Here First: The Epic of the American Indian*, 1949; Carey McWilliams, *North from Mexico: The Spanish-Speaking People of the United States*, 1949; Adolph B. Benson and Naboth Hedin, *Americans from Sweden*, 1950; Leola Bergmann, *Americans from Norway*, 1950; and J. Saunders Redding, *They Came in Chains: Americans from Africa*, 1950.

546 *Iz dveh domovin: Izjave—Reportaže—Slovstvo* [From Two Homelands]. Translated by Ivan Crnagoj, Vito Krajger, Olga Skerlj-Grahor, and Branko Rudolf. Maribor: Založba "Obzorja," 1951. Contains "The Enigma" and selections from *Laughing in the Jungle*, *My America*, *From Many Lands*, and *A Nation of Nations*.

547 *The Eagle and the Roots*. New York: Doubleday, 1952. Published posthumously. Edited by Stella Adamic and Timothy Seldes.

547a *Orel in korenine*. Translated by Mira Mihelič. Ljubljana: Državna založba Slovenije, 1970. Introduction by Ivan Bratko.

III. Forewords and Other Minor Contributions to Pamphlets and Books

548 Letter to Borden R. Purcell, Whiting Senior High School, Whiting, Indiana, in answer to a Purcell request for a preface, in *Leisure Reading Program for Whiting High School* (Whiting, Indiana, 1939), p. 6.

549 Louis Adamic's statement, in Committee on Citizenship for Younghill Kang, *Citizenship for Younghill Kang* (New York: Committee on Citizenship for Younghill Kang, 1939, [p. 4].

550 "Savo Radulovic," an introduction to *Paintings by Savo Radulovic* (New York: A.C.A. Gallery, 1940), pp. 1-2.

551 "After Nineteen Years," in Marston Balch, ed., *Modern Short Biographies and Autobiographies* (New York: Harcourt, Brace, 1940), pp. 116-147.

552 Foreword to Leonard Austin, *Around the World in San Francisco* (Stanford: James Ladd Delkin, 1940), p. iii.

553 "Alexander of Yugoslavia," in Lawrence Fernsworth, ed., *Dictators and Democrats* (New York: McBride, 1941), pp. 187-198.

554 "By Louis Adamic," in Robert Spiers Benjamin, ed., *I Am an American: By Famous Naturalized Americans* (New York: Alliance Book Corp., 1941), pp. 76-82.

555 "Louis Adamic: Why He Selected 'Girl on the Road,' " in Whit Burnett, ed., *This Is My Best* (New York: Dial Press, 1942), p. 483.

556 "The Living Affirmation of Democracy of Louis Adamic," in Norman Cousins, ed., *A Treasury of Democracy* (New York: Coward-McCann, 1942), pp. 151-153.

557 Introduction, signed by Adamic and nine others, to *The Truth about Yugoslavia: A Documentary Record* (Pittsburgh: Miko Markovich, 1943), p. 3.

558 "My America, My World: Louis Adamic," in Robert M. Bartlett, *They Work for Tomorrow* (New York: Association Press, 1943), pp. 21-31. An interview-compilation by Bartlett.

559 Foreword to Rachel DuBois (Davis), *Get Together Americans: Friendly Approaches to Racial and Cultural Conflicts Through Neighborhood-Home Festival* (New York and London: Harper, 1943), p. ix.

560 Facsimile of typescript letter, on cover of Nalley's Inc., *This Is the Beginning: The Story of Nalley's, Written by and for the Men and Women of the Nalley's Organization.* Tacoma, Washington: Nalley's, 1944.

561 Introduction to Ivor Thomas, M.P., and Mato Vučetič, *The Italo-Jugoslav Frontier* (Chicago: Slovenian American National Council, [1944]), p. 2.

562 Introduction to Josip Broz Tito, *The Yugoslav Peoples Fight to Live* (New York: United Committee of South-Slavic Americans, 1944), pp. 3-4.

563 Foreword to Associated American Artists Galleries, *Lionel Reiss' Manhattan Crosstown* (New York: Associated American Artists Galleries, May, 1946), p. 2.

564 "From Plymouth Rock to Ellis Island," an introduction to Harry Shaw and Ruth Davis, eds., *Americans One and All* (New York and London: Harper, 1947), pp. xiii-xviii.

IV. Portions of Books Reprinted in Pamphlets and Books by Others

565 "Pittsburgh, June 20," in *The Great American Parade* (New York: Doubleday, Doran, 1935), pp. 559-572. From *Dynamite.*

556 "An Incident," in *Nazi Poison: How We Can Destroy Hitler's Propaganda Against the Jews.* Democracy in Action No. 8 (New York: Council for Democracy, 1941), pp. 2-3. From *Two-Way Passage.*

567 "My America" [a portion of *My America*] and "Mr. Adamic wrote this in a letter to Paul. . . ," in National Broadcasting Company, *I Believe in America* (New York: National Broadcasting Company, 1941), [pp. 14-15]. The pamphlet *I Believe in America* advertised the patriotism of the Barbour family, the characters of Carlton E. Morse's popular radio serial *One Man's Family.*

568 "Girl on the Road," in Whitt Burnett, ed., *This Is My Best* (New York: Dial Press, 1942), pp. 483-510. From *My America.*

568a "Dekle s ceste," *Obzornik*, VI, 10 (1951), 596-613. Translated by Olga Grahor.

569 "The Man in a Quandary," in Shlomo Bardin, ed., *Self-Fulfillment Through Zionism: A Study in Jewish Adjustment.* Study Group Unit No. 3 (New York: American Zionist Youth Commission, [1943]), pp. 45-64. From *From Many Lands.*

570 "A Dying Guerrilla's Testament," in Curt Riess, ed., *They Were There: The Story of World War II and How It Came About by America's Foremost Correspondents* (New York: G. P. Putnam's, 1944), pp. 617-619. From *My Native Land.*

V. Special Materials in the Princeton University Library

571 Typescript of translation: "A Village Cyrano," by Anton Novačhan.

572 Typescript of translation: "Glimpses of My Childhood," by Ivan Cankar.

573 Typescript of translation: "The Way of the Cross," by Ivan Cankar.

574 Typescript of translation: "The Goal," by Ivan Cankar.

575 "The Literature of Labor." Mimeographed text of a Columbia Broadcasting System Labor Day, 1933, radio interview of Louis Adamic by Mr. Stix.

576 Mimeograph of the February 28, 1934, broadcast of "The Italics are Mine"—a weekly radio program presented over W.O.R., New York City, 9:15–9:45 p.m., featuring H. Stokes Lott, Jr. The February 28 broadcast presented Lott speaking about and quoting from Adamic's *The Native's Return*, especially the chapter "Death Waits for My Uncle Yanez."

577 File cards for presentation, with revisions, of "A Country Full of Nice People," a speech delivered under the auspicies of The Modern Forum at Philharmonic Auditorium, Los Angeles, April 13, 1936, 8 p.m., and

elsewhere during the Spring of 1936. The final form of this speech became "A Lecture By Louis Adamic." *See below* no. 578.

578 "A Lecture By Louis Adamic." A broadsheet, printed on both sides, nineteen by eighteen inches, ca. 1936.

579 Typed sheets [backs of Hotel Hollenden, Cleveland, stationery] representing the major portion of a speech concerning the possibility of labor and business joining for common good. ca. 1936.

580 A typed, edited MS., of "Louis Adamic's talk . . . Progressive Education Association Conference," Washington, D. C., February 21, 1936.

581 Fifteen typed and nine autograph pages of Ms. of speech "30,000,000" ("Thirty Million New Americans"). ca. 1936.

582 Typescripts of "Chichicastenango": "1st draft, pp. 1-20, final" with autograph revisions; second draft with autograph revisions; and a carbon of second draft after revisions.

583 Mimeograph of questionnaire "To Former Students of Antioch College," dated November 10, 1937.

584 "Slovenskim podpornim organizacijam v Ameriki," signed and dated by Adamic.

585 "The following is a suggestion in a letter from one of my correspondents:" A form letter on Louis Adamic stationery, distributed to those on Adamic's mailing list, suggesting that peoples of mixed ethnic and racial background consciously join together at least "to rub shoulders" if not exchange ideas.

586 A form letter on Louis Adamic stationery answering requests for information about the correct pronounciation of *Adamic*.

587 Typescript and carbon copy of "Ellis Island in Reverse."

588 A typescript copy with autograph revisions of a memorandom to Frederick P. Keppel, President of the Carnegie Corporation, dated October 1, 1938.

589 Carbon typescript of "Summery of a Lecture by Louis Adamic" with a note attached stating "This lecture is an integral part of the method and mechanics of the project—I deliver it here and there, off and on."

590 A form letter addressed and dated "To Distinguished Immigrant Americans: June, 1939" to accompany Adamic's broadside questionnaire "Plymouth Rock and Ellis Island." Other letters of the same nature but with appropriate changes for "To Polish Americans: July 20, 1939," "To Italian Americans: November, 1939," "To Finnish Americans: Winter, 1939," "To Jewish Americans," "To a Selected List of People Known To Be Interested. . . ," "To Those Whose Names Were Sent By Mr. Edward Edick," and so forth.

591 Mimeograph of "Plymouth Rock and Ellis Island: Summary of a Lecture," with instructions to editors of newspapers to which Adamic sent it.

592 A mimeograph of "Let's Become Americanized—ALL OF US." Title page reads in part: "Rough Draft—to be revised, perhaps entirely rewritten. Confidential—Not for publication or quotation in this version, not for public comment. To be read only by the person to whom addressed. (Copyright 1939 Louis Adamic)."

593 Carbon typescript with autograph revisions of "A Nation Of Nations: A brief synopsis of, or suggestion for, a two- or three-reel motion picture dealing with the rich variety of the racial and national strains of the population of the U.S.—the picture to be produced by the School System of New York City, primarily for school use—Prepared at the request of Mr. James Marshall, President, Board of Education of the City of New York." ca. 1939.

594 Mimeograph of "Request For Facts and Views On The 'Negro Problem' "; reprinted, edited, from the *North Georgia Review*. Fall 1939.

595 Advertisement for Louis Adamic's "Let's Become Americanized—All of Us" speech on Friday, October 27, 1939, 8 p.m., at Community Playhouse, San Francisco, sponsored by the International Institute (A Community Chest Agency), bearing Adamic's notes on the backgrounds of the sponsors of the evening.

596 Typescript of "Lecture Before Adult Education, May 21, 1940, Astor Hotel, N. Y. C." Original title was "Apropos the Fifth Column."

597 Mimeograph of "I'm An American!" Script No. 15: a conversation between Mr. Shaughnessy, Deputy Commissioner of the Immigration and Naturalization Service, and Louis Adamic; WEAF—National Broadcasting Company, New York, Saturday, August 10, 1940, 1:00–1:15 p.m. E.S.T.

598 Typescript with autograph revisions of "Radio Speech, November 13, [1940?], 4:15 p.m., WOL, Washington, D. C."

599 Foreword to The 1942 Class of Theodore Roosevelt High School, *Are We Americans? A History of Our Ancestors* (Des Moines, Iowa: The 1942 Class, 1940), p. 4. Carbon typescript, bound.

600 Typescript with autograph revisions of "Tired Radical."

601 A Harper & Bros. advertisement for *Two-Way Passage* announcing a previously unscheduled publication for October 19, 1941, and quoting Adamic.

602 A four page advertisement for *Two-Way Passage* including an order blank addressed to Adamic for inscribed copies. By 1937 such advertisements were common for all of Adamic's books.

603 "A Statement by—Louis Adamic"—an answer to a letter from a woman in Gary, Indiana—printed on the first page of a four page advertisement for *Two-Way Passage* bearing the notation "THIS CIRCULAR is being sent to a limited list of Mr. Adamic's friends and correspondents."

604 Mimeograph of an Eleanor Roosevelt-Louis Adamic single exchange of letters concerning *Two-Way Passage.*

605 Mimeograph script of "Treasury Star Parade" radio program of June 7, 1942: A John Latouche drama suggested by Louis Adamic's book *Two-Way Passage,* starring Paul Henried and Fay Bainter.

606 Carbon typescripts, some with autograph revisions, of Louis Adamic's work on a film for King Vidor, Spring, 1942, including: "Woman with Lamp," "Woman with The Torch," "U.S.A.," "Second Panel—U.S.A.," "The Big Journey."

607 "It Isn't Peanuts." Mimeograph of the Malcolm Meacham radio adaptation of the Adamic story, presented on "The Treasury Star Parade," September 15, 1942, Record No. 102.

608 Mimeographed text of "Louis Adamic's Address at the Reichstag Fire Trial Anniversary Mass Meeting in Carnegie Hall, December 22, 1943."

609 Mimeograph of Adamic's formal statement of resignation and documentation of reasons thereof from the Common Council for American Unity, dated March 1, 1944.

610 Mimeograph of "Louis Adamic's Address at the Book and Author Luncheon given by the New York Herald Tribune on March 7, 1944," from the United Committee of South-Slavic Americans.

611 Mimeograph of "For Immediate Release": an Adamic press release via the United Committee of South-Slavic Americans stating that Adamic had received what was believed to be the first letter from Tito to anyone in the United States; the letter was dated March 29, 1944, but had been received some time later.

612 A carbon typescript of a December 17, 1945, letter to Nick Bez which includes a transcript, in typical Adamic style, of Adamic's December 6 interview of President Harry S. Truman on the subject of Yugoslavia.

613 Mimeograph copy for distribution of Adamic's letter to James F. Byrnes. Mimeograph copy of same letter translated into Slovenian. English version became the pamphlet *America and Trieste: God and the Russians.*

614 Pages from Louis Adamic's day book for January, February, and March 1945.

615 Autograph copy of "American-Russian Relations": an address delivered at a meeting sponsored by the Chicago Council of American-Soviet Friendship, March 9, 1947.

616 Carbon typescript of "Louis Adamic's Lecture: October–November, 1947."

617 Carbon typescript with autograph revisions of "Brief Outline of 'The Education of Michael Novak.' "

618 Carbon typescript with revisions of "A Lecture By Louis Adamic—now (Feb.–March) being delivered in various American cities and towns." Differs from no. 619 *below*.

619 Mimeograph of "A Lecture By Louis Adamic—now (Feb.–March) being delivered in various American cities and towns. Tentative Draft," with comments by an unidentified person.

620 Cards for presentation of a speech on tolerance.

621 Typescript and autograph revision of "America and Yugoslavia: A lecture: first delivered before The Forum in Philadelphia on January 19, 1947, and during February and March before audiences in other parts of the United States."

622 "Who's Who In The Greek Government." A carbon typescript of an address by Louis Adamic, prepared for delivery before the National Conference on American Policy in Greece in New York City on January 4, 1948.

623 Typescript with autograph revisions of a speech (ca. 1948) titled "America and Yugoslavia, And The Larger World Crisis." This bears editing by a second person.

624 A carbon typescript of "Apropos of Louis Budenz' attempt to drag him into the current hysteria wave, Louis Adamic issued the following statement:" (1948). Adamic's reaction to Budenz' remarks received general news coverage, but lengthy quotations from Adamic's full statement were rare. Even the translation "Louis Adamič zavrgel izjave Budenza," *Enakopravnost* (Cleveland), August 6, 1948, p. 1, is an edited version.

625 A mimeographed letter on Louis Adamic stationery, dated mid-June, 1948, and addressed to the "3,500 current subscribers to T & T," asking for contributions to raise $1,000 to allow 10,000 extra copies of a *T & T* issue on Henry Wallace to be printed.

626 Carbon typescript of "Were I now running for a high office this year as a progressive, I'd say something like this in one of my speeches:"

627 Carbon typescript of "Letter to Louis Adamic from Lee Fryer, executive assistant to Jim Patton, of the National Farmers Union, Denver . . . with Remarks by Louis Adamic," dated Denver, July 10, [1948].

628 A carbon typescript of "An Address by Louis Adamic." A speech supporting Henry Wallace, 1948.

629 Mimeograph of a draft of the Progressive Party Platform of 1948, a mimeograph of a differing draft of the Platform titled "Draft Platform: Confidential," and a mimeograph of a draft titled " 'Peace, Freedom and Abundance': For Release p.m. Saturday 7/24/48." On August 7, 1948, Adamic wrote to a friend: "I was one of the 5 people who wrote the platform, or rather the next-to-the-final draft of it; and we had to be in Philadelphia four days

ahead of the opening of the convention. As it turned out, we should have been working on the draft five *weeks* before, not five days. The final document runs to about 7000 words, and it was some job. The writing of it was just about the most *democratic*—that is to say, difficult—thing I've ever been mixed up in. The over-all Platform Committee consisted of 70–odd people, of whom 60–odd were present at most meetings, each with several ideas. All these people had to be satisfied, more or less. Besides, we invited the whole country, the sane and the crackpot parts of it, to come and present ideas before a special committee of the Platform Committee which sat for 2 days, almost day and night, and listened to the proposals, which were then conveyed to the full Committee and finally to us five who were writing the document. . . . I never went through anything like it. Outside our door were 80 reporters day and night. They almost physically assailed the girls who served as our messengers carrying pages of the draft platform to the mimeograph room. The girls had to hide the pages under their clothing. The mimeograph room was guarded; none of the people in that room went out of it for nearly three days, sleeping on the floor. The draft had to be finished by Saturday morning [July 24], so that it could be passed out in mimeographed form to the 3000 delegates in the afternoon." The final draft of the Platform was published as *Peace, Freedom and Abundance: The Platform of the Progressive Party, 1948*, New York: Progressive Party, 1948; and translated as *Mir Svoboda in Izobilje*, Chicago: Slovenian American National Council—Slovenian Americans for Wallace, 1948; and as a single issue newspaper titled *Mir, Sloboda I Obilje*.

630 Typescript with autograph revisions of "War and Peace."

VI. Special Materials in Narodna in Univerzitetna Knjiznica, Ljubljana, Yugoslavia

631 Mimeograph of the March 9, 1934, WJZ and Blue Network interview by Mr. Lundell of Louis and Stella Adamic.

632 Typescript with autograph revisions of an introduction to a collection of Yugoslav short stories in translation which Adamic hoped to publish as a single volume. Not all the the translations were by Adamic. ca. 1936.

633 A mimeographed "Memorandum" dated July 1, 1944, addressed to selected Yugoslav Americans asking for suggestions on the text of the article "Americans from Yugoslavia" and requesting the matter be considered "confidential until the article appears next December or January." A mimeograph of "Americans from Yugoslavia" is attached.

634 "Appeal for Used Clothing and Blankets for Liberated Yugoslavia." A circular, signed by Louis Adamic, sponsored by the War Relief Fund of Americans of South-Slavic Descent, eight and one half inches by eight inches, ca. Autumn, 1945.

VII. A Selected List of Biographical and Critical Materials about Louis Adamic

635 "Književne novosti," *Prosveta*, May 19, 1926, p. 3.

636 Roberts, W. Adolphe. "Without a Policy," *The American Parade*, I (July 1926), 6.

637 M[olek], I[van]. "Cankarjev 'Hlapec Jernej' izšel v angleščini," *Prosveta*, September 1, 1926, p. 2.

638 Vidmar, Josip. " 'Hlapec Jernej' v angleščini," *Jutro* (Ljubljana), VII, 216 (1926), 11.

639 "Yerney's Justice . . . Adamič . . . ," *Priloga časa* (Cleveland), XII, 9 (1926), 65.

640 Hennessy, Dan. "Haldeman-Julius Writers," *Haldeman-Julius Monthly*, VI (July, 1927), 106-107.

641 "Adamic Again in the Mercury," *Prosveta*, August 22, 1927, p. 6.

642 McWilliams, Carey. "Southern California Begins to Write: I. Louis Adamic: Ex-Crusader," *Saturday Night*, October 22, 1927, pp. 4-5.

643 Kobal, A[ndrej]. "Ne pljuvati v lastno skledo!" *Prosveta*, July 25, 1928, p. 2.

643a "Pljuvanje v Lastno Skledo," *Glasilo Kranjsko-Slovenske Katoliške Jednote* (Cleveland), August 14, 1928, p. 4.

643a* *Enakopravnost* (Cleveland), August 15, 1928, p. 2.

644 "Editorial Notes," *American Mercury*, xiv (July, 1928), xxviii, xxx.

645 Molek, Ivan. "Opazovanja," *Prosveta*, August 22, 1928, p. 4.

646 Imp. "Louis Adamic," *Srpski književni glasnik*, N.S. xxiv, 6 (1928), 476-477. Cyr.

647 McWilliams, Carey. "Robinson Jeffers: An Antitoxin," *Saturday Night*, August 3, 1929, p. 5.

648 "A Roster of Los Angeles 'Liberals,' " *Bulletin: Better America Federation of California*, x (December 13, 1928), 2.

649 Conroy, Jack. "Ford of Literature," *Outlook and Independent*, clv (August 27, 1930), 679.

650 DeCaluwe, E.G. "Defending Mr. Adamic," *Outlook and Independent*, clv (September 10, 1930), 80.

651 Haldeman-Julius, E. "Mr. Haldeman-Julius Enters the Ring," *Outlook and Independent*, clv (September 10, 1930), 80.

652 " 'Woodrow Wilson Slain,' According to I.W.W. 'Assassin,' " New York *Inquirer*, September 28, 1930, pp. 1, 2.

653 "The Roots of Racketeering," *The New Freeman*, ii (March 4, 1931), 582, 584.

654 Rowell, Chester. "Current Comment," Los Angeles *Evening Express*, March 6, 1931, p. 12.

655 Hardman, J.B.S. "Dynamite! . . . that's the Stuff!" *The Advance*, XVII (March 20, 1931), 1, 6.

656 Budenz, Louis Francis. "Violence in the Class War," *Labor Age*, XX (March, 1931), 25-26.

657 Godwin, Murray. "Apology for Ford," *The New Freeman*, III (April 15, 1931), 105-107.

658 ———. "For My Friend Louis Adamic," *The New Freeman*, III (April 29, 1931), 160-161.

659 "News from Nowhere," *Contempo*, I (May, 1931), 3.

660 O'Flaherty, Tom. "To the Editors of *Contempo*," *Contempo*, I (July, 1931), 2.

661 Billy, Hill. "Economic Fiction," Portland *News Telegram*, October 6, 1931.

662 Winchell, Walter. "Walter Winchell On Broadway," New York *Daily Mirror*, November 30, 1931, p. 23.

663 Labor Research Association. "A Factual Correction," *Contempo*, I (December 1, 1931), 3.

664 Winchell, Walter. "Walter Winchell On Broadway," New York *Daily Mirror*, December 4, 1931, p. 31.

665 Pass, Joseph. "Communist vs. Adamic," *Contempo*, I (December 15, 1931), 1.

666 Announcement of Adamic's article on Clarence Darrow which was later refused. *Atlantic Monthly*, CXLVIII (December, 1931), 2.

667 [Angjelinovic, Berislav]. "Istaknuti naši ljudi u životu Amerike," *Jugoslovenski almanak* (New York, 1931), p. 14.

668 Klakočer, L[udvik]. "Dynamite . . . 1931," *Dom in svet*, XLIV, 7-9 (1931), 410-413.

669 Klopčič, M[ile]. "Veliko književno delo ameriškega Slovenca," *Jutro* (Ljubljana), XII, 83 (1931), 6.

670 "Lujo Adamič," *Narodna zaštita*, XV, 3 (1931), 9.

671 [Mrzel, Ludvik]. "Slovenec—ameriški pisatelj," *Jugoslovan*, II, 83 (1931), 7.

672 "Slovenac—američki književnik," *Slobodna tribuna*, XI, 919 (1931), 5.

673 Skerlj, O[lga]. "Louis Adamič . . . 1931," *Ljubljanski Zvon*, LII (January, 1932), 57-62.

673a "Slovenska kritika o 'Dinamitu,' " *15 dana: Kronika naše kulture* (Zagreb), III (July, 1933), 197-198.

674 "Finds United States Much Like a Jungle: Adamic's New Book Pictures Chaos Here That Calls for Acute Sense of Humor," New York *Times*, March 23, 1932, p. 19.

675 "Land of Promise," New York *Times*, March 27, 1932, Sec. IV, pp. 21, 23.

676 M[olek], I[van]. "Adamič odkril Ameriko," *Prosveta*, April 8, 1932, p. 2; April 9, p. 2.

677 "Books and Persons: Louis Adamich in Belgrade. . . ," *South Slav Herald*, June 1, 1932, p. 5.

678 Frigid [Ludvik Mrzel]. "Srečanje z Louisom Adamičem," *Prosveta*, June 6, 1932, p. 3.

679 Klopčič, Mile. "Srečenja in pogovori s pisateljem Louisom Adamičem," *Prosveta*, June 20, 1932, p. 3; July 8, p. 3.

680 Frigid. Mrzel, L[udvik]. "Kriza v Ameriki. Ob novi knjigi Louisa Adamiča," *Prosveta*, September 17, 1932, p. 3.

681 Zupančič, Oton. "Adamič in slovenstvo," *Ljubljanski Zvon*, LII (September, 1932), 513-520.

681a *15 dana: Kronika naše kulture* (Zagreb), II, 21 (1932), 323-324.

681b "Adamic and Slovenism," translated by Joseph Zelle, *The American Slav*, F (December, 1939), 21-32; G (February, 1940), 12-13.

682 Albrecht, Fran, Ferdo Kozak, Stanko Leben, Josip Vidmar, and Lojze Udè. *Kriza: Ljubljanskega zvona*. Ljubljana: Tiskarna "Slovenija," 1932.

683 A-a. "K sporu za slovenstvo," *Slovenija* (Ljubljana), I, 19 (1932), 3.

684 Bauer, Ruben. "Louis Adamič: Smijeh u džungli . . . 1932," *Hanoar* (Zagreb), VI, 4-5 (1932–1933), 137.

685 "Ein amerikanischer Schriftsteller in Zagreb," *Morgenblatt*, XLVII, 143 (1932), 2.

686 Horvat, Mladen. "Dva romana o Americi: Luis Adamič i Agnes Smedley i njihova dela," *Zivot i rad*, V, knj. XIII, 78 (1932), 1636–1637. Cyr.

687 [Horvath, Josip]. "Optužba naše savjesti. Adamičeva knjiga 'Smijeh u džungli.' Potresna istina o životu naših seljaka u Americi," *Jutarnji list* (Zagreb), XXI, 7449 (1932), 7.

687a *Novi iseljenik*, XI, 11 (1932), 6.

688 "Jugosloven-američki romansijer. Ljubljana, 22 maja," *Politika*, XXIX, 8633 (1932), 6. Cyr.

689 "Yugosloven koji je postao slavan književnik u Americi," *Radio Beograd*, IV, 25 (1932), 24. Cyr.

690 Klakočer, L[udvik]. "Laughing in the Jungle . . . 1932," *Dom in svet*, XLV, 7-8 (1932), 329-330.

691 K[lop]čič, M[ile]. "Nov spis Louisa Adamiča," *Jutro* (Ljubljana), XIII, 106 (1932), 6.

692 K[očevar], C[iril]. "Louis Adamič o sebi in domovini," *Slovenec* (Ljubljana), LX, 112 (1932), 2.

693 Kunin, V. "Louis Adamič: Smeh u džungli," *Jugoslovenska reč*, I, 12 (1932), 3-4.

694 "Louis Adamič o svom životu," *15 dana: Kronika naše kulture* (Zagreb), II, 11 (1932), 173-174.

695 Ložar, Rajko. "Kaj bi bilo, če bi bilo," *Dom in svet*, XLV, 7-8 (1932), 320-328.

696 Mašic, Br[anko]. "Novi književni izražaj na pomolu. Povodom Louis Adamičevog djela 'Smjeh u džungli,' " *Novosti* (Zagreb), XXVI, 355 (1932), 30-31.

697 M. "Louis Adamič v domovini. Naš rojak, ugledni ameriški pisatelj, ki si je pridobil sloves zlasti s svojo knjigo 'Dinamit,' o svojih vtisih v domovini," *Slovenski narod* (Ljubljana), LXV, 117 (1932), 3.

698 [Mihovilovic, Ive]. "Naši, koji se u svijetu uspinju," *Novosti* (Zagreb), XXVI, 146 (1932), 11.

699 Nevistic, I[van]. "Roman našega 'Amerikanca' . . . 1932," *Pravda* (Beograd), XXVIII, 310, (1932), 6. Cyr.

700 "Oton Zupančič na bramiku notranjega slovenstva," *Slovenec* (Ljubljana), LX, 221 (1932), 7.

701 Potokar, Tone. "Cetiri eseja našeg zemljaka Adamiča, poznatog američkog književnika. Luis Adamič, pisac 'Dinamita,' o životu u Novom Svetu," *Politika*, XXIX, 8778 (1932), 10. Cyr.

702 P[otokar], T[one]. "Louis Adamič: 'Kriza u Ameriki,' " *Srpski književni glasnik*, N.S. XXXVII, 2 (1932), 151.

703 ———. "Luis Adamič u Beogradu," *Politika*, XXIX, 8634 (1932), 7. Cyr.

704 ———. "Louis Adamič u Dubrovniku," *15 dana: Kronika naše kulture* (Zagreb), II, 21 (1932), 324.

705 ———. "Luis Adamič: Zena iz Dalmacije," *Srpski književni glasnik*, N.S. XXXVII, 4 (1932), 319.

706 "Prokletstvo mamonizma. Louis Adamič o Ameriki," *Slovenec* (Ljubljana), LX, 117 (1932), 2.

707 "Razkrinkana pravljica o obljubljeni Ameriki. Louis Adamič: 'Kriza v Ameriki,' " *Mariborski večernik "Jutra,"* VI, 183 (1932), 5.

708 Sestak, Ivan. "Smijeh u džungli," *Evolucija*, I, 13 (1932), 986-987.

709 [Skerl, Silvester]. "Louis Adamič: Krizi v Ameriki," *Slovenec* (Ljubljana), LX, 183 (1932), 7.

710 [Teply, Bogo]. "Louis Adamič: Kriza v Ameriki," *Svoboda*, IV, 11 (1932), 361.

711 Vek—. "Nekaj opomb k Zupančičevemu pojmovanju naših sedanjih problemov," *Slovenija* (Ljubljana), I, 12 (1932), 1-2.

712 "Velik uspeh Louisa Adamiča v Ameriki," *Jutro* (Ljubljana), XIII, 78 (1932), 5.

713 Z[imbrek], L[adislav]. "Louis Adamič," *Novosti* (Zagreb), XXVI, 234 (1932), 9; 235 (1932), 9.

714 B., V. "Louis Adamič o životu i Literature," *Novosti Broj 27*, January 27, 1933.

715 ———. "Novi Adamičev roman," *Novosti Broj 28*, January 28, 1933.

716 Kozak, Ferdo. "Zgrešena polemika," *Sodobnost*, I, 1 (1933), 29-31.

717 H[arambaši]č, Z[arko]. "Kaos Amerike—zemlje gigantskih dimenzija," *Jutarnji list (Zagreb)*, February 2, 1933, pp. 7-8.

718 K[lopčič], M[ile]. "Louis Adamič o življenju in literaturi. Razgovor z ameriškim rojakom, pisateljem Adamičem o Ameriki in njeni literaturi," *Prosveta*, February 16, 1933, p. 4; "Novi roman Louisa Adamiča 'The Darkened Plain,' roman o sedanji krizi," February 17, p. 4.

719 V[idmar], J[osip]. "Pod Vrazovo senco," *Sodobnost*, I (February, 1933), 96.

720 ———. "Veliko vprašanje," *Sodobnost*, I (February, 1933), 79-80.

721 "Louis Adamič se vrnil nazaj v Ameriko," *Prosveta*, April 11, 1933, pp. 1, 3.

722 Mrzel, L[udvik]. "Kulturni pregled: Roman slovenskega izseljenca," *Jutro* (Ljubljana), April 21, 1933, pp. 3-4.

723 Kalan, Filip. "Louis Adamič: Smeh v džungli . . . Ljubljani 1933," *Modra ptica*, IV (June, 1933), 222-223.

724 "Američki glasovi o 'Dinamitu,' " *15 dana: Kronika naše kulture* (Zagreb), III (July, 1933), 199.

725 "Yugoslav Terror Is Told by Article," *Slavic (American) News* (Los Angeles), August 17, 1933, p. 1.

726 L[eben], S[tanko]. "Pismo iz Jugoslavije," *Sodobnost*, I (August, 1933), 383-384.

727 "Magazines, Lectures, Radio and Trial Occupy Adamic's Time," *Enakopravnost* (Cleveland), September 14, 1933.

728 "Komentarji: Naši notranji problemi. Adamič naletel na sršene," *Prosveta*, October 4, 1933, p. 1.

729 "Nepredni somišljenik stare Vatikanske 'Rote,' " *Slovenski Belgrajski Teduék*, October 15, 1933, p. 1.

730 "Adamic's New Book," *Prosveta*, November 15, 1933, p. 7.

731 "Današnji Beograd," *Svyet*, November 17, 1933.

732 "Komentarji: Praznovenje v starem Kraju," *Prosveta*, November 17, 1933, p. 1.

733 "Adamič izzval oster ameriški protest proti Jugoslaviji," *Prosveta*, November 28, 1933, p. 1.

734 Hugo, P. "Louis Adamiča 'Smrt na Kranjskem,' " *Amerikanski Slovenec*, November 28, 1933, p. 2.

734a *Slovenec* (Ljubljana), LXI, 287 (1933), 3.

735 "Jedno pismo," *Svijet* (New York), November 29, 1933, p. 2.

736 Grahor, Olga. "Smeh v džungli . . . Ljubljani 1933," *Ljubljanski Zvon*, LIII (November, 1933), 692-695; (December), 750-752.

737 "Jugoslav Affairs," *Enakopravnost* (Cleveland), December 23, 1933.

738 "Sijajno Priznanje za Adamiče vo Knjigo o Jugoslaviji," *Enakopravnost* (Cleveland), December 23, 1933, p. 1.

739 "Adamic's Book Out Feb. 1," *Prosveta*, December 27, 1933, p. 6.

740 Lupis-Vukic, I[vo] F[rano]. "Kako se kod nas prevodi," *Nova Evropa*, XXVI (December, 1933), 555-561.

741 " 'Dinamit': Al Capone i njegovi gangsteri u jednom drugom svjetlu," *Hrvatski list*, XIV, 180 (1933), 5-6.

742 Drainac, Rade. "E, nije tako! Slovenci kroz prizmu američkih 'levičarskih' pisaca," *Pravda* (Beograd), XXIX, 10244 (1933), 5. Cyr.

743 L., I. "Misli ob Adamičevi knjiga 'Smeh v džungli,' " *Pohod* (Ljubljana), II, 17 (1933), 2-3.

744 N., I. "Stare vatikanske 'rote.' Povodom slučaja književnika L. Adamiča," *Pravda* (Beograd), XXIX, 10375, (1933), 7. Cyr.

745 Jevtic, M[ilan]. "Za 65 dolara samo!" *Banatski glasnik*, XVI, 41 (1933), 3. Cyr.

746 [Jugovar, Beno], and [Bogo Teply]. "Polemika o Adamičevi knjigi 'Kriza v Ameriki,' " *Svoboda*, V, 1 (1933), 46-47.

747 "Lojze Adamič ob slovesu. Ponarejene njegove izjave," *Slovenec* (Ljubljana), LXI, 72 (1933), 3.

748 "Louis Adamič u Zagrebu," *Novi iseljenik* (Zagreb), XII, 2 (1933), 7.

749 Lupis-Vukic, I[v]o F[rane]. "Luis Adamič i—Amerika," *Novo dobo* (Split), XVI, 26 (1933), 3.

750 Peroš, V[ilim]. "Louis Adamič," *Danica*, III, 74 (1933), 4.

751 Petris, Hijacint. "Par dana s Louisom Adamičem," *15 dana: Kronika naše kulture* (Zagreb), III, 4 (1933), 55-57.

752 ———. "Adamičev 'Dinamit: Povjest klasnog nasilja'—Amerika 'džungla' pod teretom bandita i dinamita," *Novo dobo* (Split), XVI, 222 (1933), 2-3.

753 Pinto, V[iktor] B. "Iz Amerike natrag u domovinu. Utisci o književniku Louisu Adamiču i njegovi utisci o Jugoslaviji," *Jugoslavenski list*, XVI, 7 (1933), 4.

754 Silc, J[akob]. "Louis Adamič: Kriza v Ameriki . . . Ljubljana 1933," *Dom in svet*, XXXXVI, 1-2 (1933), 96.

755 ———. "Louis Adamič: Smeh v džungli . . . Ljubljani 1933," *Dom in svet*, XXXXVI, 5 (1933), 268-269.

756 [Stukelj, Ciril]. "Oton Zupančič, Louis Adamich, slovenstvo i. . . ," *Svoboda*, V, 1 (1933), 61.

757 Subic, Lujza. "Louis Adamič. Njegova mladost. Zivot u Americi. Dobrovoljac u svjetskom ratu. Novinar. Prvo djelo i uspjeh," *Jugoslavenski list*, XVI, 4 (1933), 4.

758 University of Iowa. *Literature and the Art of Writing: An Introduction to the Courses of Required English in the College of Liberal Arts and the School of Letters at the University of Iowa, 1934–1935* (Iowa City: University of Iowa, 1933), pp. 21-23.

759 "Uspjelo predavanje Louisa Adamiča. Sinoc u Hrv. glasbenom zavodu," *Večer*, XIV, 3649 (1933), 3.

760 V-ic. "Luj Adamič: Dinamit. . . ," *Zeta*, IV, 25 (1933), 3. Cyr.

761 "Pismo iz Clevelanda," *Prosveta*, January 3, 1934, p. 2.

762 "Vtisi Louis Adamiča z obiska tuj sinoči je odpotoval," *Enakopravnost* (Cleveland), January 3, 1934, p. 1.

763 "Za resnico," *Pohod* (Ljubljana), January 6, 1934, p. 3.

764 "Pismo iz Clevelanda," *Prosveta*, January 11, 1934, p. 3.

765 "Komentarji: Pisatel Adamič je v naši javnosti že osem let!" *Prosveta*, January 15, 1934, p. 1.

766 Adamic, Stella. "Mrs. Adamic's Statement," *Prosveta*, January 17, 1937, p. 8.

766a "Pismo uredništvu," *Nova Doba* (Cleveland), January 24, 1934, p. 2.

767 Slaje, Rev. Milan. " 'Death in Carniola' by Louis Adamic," *Ameriška Domovína*, January 27, 1934, p. 3.

768 "Adamičeva Knjiga 'The Native's Return,' " *Prosveta*, January 31, 1934, p. 4.

769 Cainkar, Vincent. "Read Adamic's New Book," *Prosveta*, January 31, 1934, p. 7.

770 "Louis Adamic—His Literary Career in Brief Outline," *Slovenska Narodna* (Chicago), January 31, 1934, p. 1.

770a *Nova Doba* (Cleveland), February 14, 1934, p. 6.

771 Canby, Henry S. "The Native's Return" *Book-of-the-Month Club News*, January, 1934. Includes Maurice Hindus, "Louis Adamic," p. 4.

771a *Prosveta*, January 10, 1934, p. 8.

771b "Kaj pravijo ameriški kritiki o novi Adamičevi knjigi," *Prosveta*, January 17, 1934, p. 3.

772 M., B. "Romance and Laughter Ring Out in Adamic's Book on Yugoslavia," *Slavic-American News* (Los Angeles), February 1, 1934.

773 Billich, Milan. "Urodjenikov Povratak," *Hrvatska*, February 1, 1934, p. 1; February 3, p. 1.

774 "Ogledalo Jugoslavije," *Svijet* (New York), February 1, 1934, p. 2.

775 Gedroyc-Dalbert, Janina. "Jugosławja w Epice Emigranta," *Dziennik Polski*, February 3, 1934, p. 3.

776 "Ameriška kritika pozdravlja 'The Native's Return,' " *Enakopravnost* (Cleveland), February 5, 1934.

777 F[oreign] L[anguage] I[nformation] S[ervice]. "Louis Adamic Eloadói Körutja," *Városi Elet*, February 9, 1934; *Lorain És Vidéke*, February 16; and *Amerikai Magyar Nepszava*, February 27. This Foreign Language Information Service press release announcing Adamic's first lecture tour was printed widely during February and March in various domestic foreign language newspapers; for example, as:

777a "Cyklus Prednášek Aloise Adamiče," *"New Yorske Listy,"* February 19; *Svet*, February 21; *Denni Hlasatel*, February 12; *Narod*, February 24; *Texan* (Houston), March 1; and as:

777b "Cyklus prédnášok Alojza Adamiča," *Katolicky Sokol*, February 21; *Náš Svet*, February 23; *Slovensky Občan* (Hazleton, Pennsylvania), February 23; *Slovák V Amerike*, March 12; *New Yorsky Dennik*; and as:

777c "Pan Louis Adamic w Objezdzie z Odczytami," *Dziennik Chicagoski*, February 15; *Pittsburczanin Weekly*, February 16; *Nowiny Polskie*, February 17; *Gwiazda* (Philadelphia), February 18; *"Nowa Anglja,"* February 23; *Republika-Górnik*, February 25; and as:

777d "Putovanja i predavanja Louis Adamiča," *Novi Svijet* (Chicago), February 17; and "Louis Adamic Na Turneji Kroz S.D.," *Slavic-American News* (Los Angeles), February 22; and "Turneja Louis Adamica," *Svijet* (New York), February 25; and in revised form in Cyrillic in *Pravda*, February 23; *Russky Golos*, March 3; *Paccbet*, March 21; *Svit*, March 29; *Amerikanskiz Russiz Viestnik*, March 29; *Novoye Russkoye Slovo* (New York), March 29; and *Pravda*, April 3.

778 Hrvatica. "Osvrt na knjigu: The Native's Return," *Novi Svijet*, February 24, 1934, p. 1.

779 A Native of Croatia. "The Native's Return," *"Zajedničar"* (Youngstown), February 28, 1934, p. 2.

780 [Curčin, Milan]. "Veliki uspeh Adamičeve knjige," *Nova Evropa*, XXVII (February, 1934), 64.

781 [Notice of Adamic's Speech at the Conference on Immigration Policy], *Folk-News* (New York), No. 35 (March 1, 1934), 2.

782 "Pomen Adamičevega dela," *Enakopravnost* (Cleveland), March 5, 1934, p. 2.

783 "Vlada kliče Louis Adamiča v Washington na posvetovanje," *Enakopravnost* (Cleveland), March 5, 1934 p. 1.

784 "Pomembno posvetovanje vladnih predstavnikov a pisateljem Adamičen," *Enakopravnost* (Cleveland), March 9, 1934, p. 1.

785 "Adamič v Washington," *Enakopravnost* (Cleveland), March 10, 1934, p. 2.

786 Howell, Ruth. "Louis Adamic Wrote a Best Seller, So U.S. Asked Him About Something Else," Washington (D. C.) *Daily News*, March 10, 1934, p. 10.

787 "Sve ovisi o tome kako ce se izvesti," *Svijet* (New York), March 10, 1934, p. 2.

788 "Adamič predložil važne sugestije v Washingtonu," *Prosveta*, March 12, 1934, p. 1.

789 "Adamičeva sugestija vladi glede kolektivnih farm za brezposelne delavce," *Prosveta*, March 14, 1934, p. 1.

790 "Adamic Pictures His Native Land: Author Gives Talks on Yugoslavia to Two Groups Here," *State Gazette* (Trenton), March 16, 1934, p. 2.

791 "Lojze Adamič," *Glas naroda*, March 16, 1934, p. 2.

792 "Un livre américain sur la Yougoslavie," *La Bulgarie* (Sofia), March 16, 1934, p. 2.

793 "Book Barred by Belgrade: Adamic's 'The Native's Return' on Proscribed List," New York *Times*, March 17, 1934, p. 13.

794 Lovcenski, Guslar. "Na peškeš Adamiču Juju," *Amerikanski Srbobran* (Pittsburgh), March 17, 1934, p. 2. Cyr.

795 "Jedan ukaz beogradskog ministra policije," *Svijet* (New York), March 18, 1934, p. 2.

796 "Adamičeva knjiga prepovedana v Jugoslaviji," *Prosveta*, March 21, 1934, p. 1.

796a *Enakopravnost* (Cleveland), March 21, 1934, p. 1.

797 "White House Calls Adamic to Give Views," Pittsburgh *Post Gazette*, March 22, 1934, p. 12.

798 "Zabrana Adamičeve knjige," *Hrvatski List I Danica Krvatska*, March 24, 1934, p. 2.

799 "Priseljenec si ogleduje svojo rojstvo domovino. Adamičeva knjiga," *Prosveta*, March 26, 1934, p. 3.

800 Harshman, Jerry. " 'You Helped Build Nation, Aid in Saving It,' Adamic Tells Audience," *The News Telegraph* (Sharon, Pennsylvania), March 26, 1934, pp. 1, 5.

801 Smaltz, Peter R. "Louis Adamic, Author of Best-Seller, Has Plans for Two More Books, He Tells Herald Writer," Sharon *Herald* (Pennsylvania), March 26, 1934, pp. 1, 7; and "Adamic's Visit Much Enjoyed by Croatians," p. 7.

802 "Adamic Says 'Melting Pot' Is Seething with Prejudice: Author Tells Hungry Club Intolerance Toward Immigrant 'Postpones Time When America Can Become Harmonious Whole,' " Pittsburgh *Post Gazette*, March 27, 1934.

803 "Anti-Alien Propaganda Hit by Yugo-Slav Speaker," Pittsburgh *Press*, March 27, 1934.

804 "Wants to Know Who Are Real Americans," Brooklyn *Daily Eagle*, March 27, 1934.

805 "Adamičeva knjiga," *Nova Doba* (Cleveland), March 28, 1934, pp. 1, 6.

806 "Adamič na predavateljski turi po Pennsylvaniji," *Enakopravnost* (Cleveland), March 30, 1934.

807 "Immigrant Author Gives Interesting Address at Sokol Hall Friday Night," *The Daily Citizen* (Ambridge, Pennsylvania), April 2, 1934.

808 "Jutri zučer predava Adamič v S. N. Domu; Vstopnina," *Enakopravnost* (Cleveland), April 2, 1934, p. 1.

809 "Italijani bi tudi radi dobil! Prevod Adamičeve knjige," *Enakopravnost* (Cleveland), April 3, 1934, p. 1.

810 "Kako nas Adamič seznanja z ameriško javnostjo," *Enakopravnost* (Cleveland), April 3, 1934, p. 2.

811 "Dynamic Louis Adamic, Leader Among Men, Speaks on Saturday at the City Club Forum," *The City* (Cleveland), XIX (April 4, 1934), 1, 6.

812 "Narod je veličastno pozdravil pisatelja Louis Adamiča," *Enakopravnost* (Cleveland), April 4, 1934, p. 1.

813 Sundic, Milovan P. "Dabl fes," *Amerikanski Srbobran* (Pittsburgh), April 5, 1934, p. 2. Cyr.

814 Hribar, Ivan. "Gospod Adamič!" *Pohod* (Ljubljana), April 7, 1934, p. 2.

815 "Kultura in g. Adamič," *"Ameriška Domovina"* (Cleveland), April 7, 1934, p. 2.

816 Steblaj, J. "To in Ono," *Enakopravnost* (Cleveland), April 7, 1934, p. 3.

817 "They Stand Out from the Crowd," *Literary Digest*, CXVII (April 7, 1934), 14.

818 "Ploskamo naj g. L. Adamiču?" *"Ameriška Domovina"* (Cleveland), April 9, 1934, p. 2.

819 C., J. "Glasovi iz naselbin: Se o Adamičevem predavanju," *Prosveta*, April 13, 1934, p. 2.

820 "Se par besed o Adamiču," *Pohod* (Ljubljana), April 14, 1934, p. 2.

821 Grdina, Josip. "Dvoličnost G. Louis Adamiča," *"Ameriška Domovina"* (Cleveland), April 17, 1934, p. 2.

822 "Kapitalizem nima socijalne vesti, pravi Adamič," *Enakopravnost* (Cleveland), April 19, 1934, p. 1 .

823 "Adamič o Mussoliniji," *"Ameriška Domovina"* (Cleveland), April 20, 1934, p. 2.

824 N-ic. "Slučaj Luisa Adamiča," *Jugoslavia* (Chicago), April 21, 1934, p. 1.

825 Silashki, Dushan D. "Adamic, A Native Fraud," *"Ameriška Domovina"* (Cleveland), April 21, 1934, p. 2.

826 "World Trade Held Sole Aim of Japanese . . . Current History Article Warns Against Fleeing. . . ," New York *Times*, April 22, 1934, Sec. II, p. 6.

827 Gray, James. "Louis Adamic To Be Heard at 'Y. W.' on 'Trip to Yugoslavia,' " St. Paul *Dispatch*, April 23, 1934.

828 "Dictator Mere Gangster, Adamic Lecture, Says," St. Paul *Dispatch*, April 24, 1934.

829 Gray, James. "Yugoslavia Charms in Adamic's Lecture," St. Paul *Pioneer Press*, April 25, 1934.

830 "An Immigrant's Viewpoint," Duluth *News-Tribune*, April 27, 1934.

831 "Kako sodijo o Louis Adamiču v domovini," "*Ameriška Domovina*" (Cleveland), May 1, 1934, pp. 1, 2.

832 "Ali so kralji 'svete in nedotakljive' osebe?" *Enakopravnost* (Cleveland), May 2, 1934, pp. 1, 2.

833 "Vesti iz življenja ameriških Slovencev," *Enakopravnost* (Cleveland), May 3, 1934, p. 1.

834 Golicic, Joe. "A Great Slovene," *Nova Doba* (Cleveland), May 9, 1934, p. 6.

835 Z., F. "Adamičevo predavanje dne 29 aprila v Milwaukeeju," *Proletarec* (Chicago), May 9, 1934, p. 3.

836 "Naručeni napadaji," *Svijet* (Chicago), May 9, 1934, p. 2.

837 Editor. "Page This, Literary Eunichs!" *Jedinstvo* (Cleveland), May 15, 1934, p. 1.

838 Historicus. " 'Struggle'—'Borba,' " *Jugoslàvenski glàsnik* (Chicago), May 17, 1934, p. 2.

839 "Louis Adamic and Moscow," *Amerikanski Srbobran* (Pittsburgh), June 19, 1934, pp. 1, 3-4.

840 VanGelder, Robert. "Books of the Times," New York *Times*, July 27, 1934, p. 15.

841 Corey, Lewis. "Class War and Violence," *Nation*, CXXXIX (August 29, 1934), 248.

842 Lerner, Tillie. "Thousand-Dollar Vagrant," *New Republic*, LXXX (August 29, 1934), 67-69.

843 "Emigrant-robotnik Słynnym Autorem Amerykańskim," *Ameryka-Echo* (Toledo), September 23, 1934, p. 2.

844 C[určin, Milan]. "Povodom Adamičeve knjige o Jugoslaviji," *Nova Evropa*, XXVII (September, 1934), 332-335.

845 "Assails Prophecies about Yugoslavia," New York *Times*, October 12, 1934, p. 22.

846 [Benedik, Louis]. "Lojzetu Adamiču," *Glas naroda,* October 16, 1934, p. 2.

847 "Consul Assails Adamic's View of Yugoslavia," New York *Herald Tribune*, October 12, 1934, p. 16.

848 Pupin, Michael. "The Yugoslav Union," New York *Times*, October 20, 1934, p. 14.

849 Tesla, Nikola. "Tribute to King Alexander," New York *Times,* October 21, 1934, Sec. IV, p. 5.

849a "Nikola Tesla o L. Adamichu," *Misel in delo*, I, 3 (1934), 46-47.

849a* "U odbranu Jugoslavije. Kralj Aleksandar Ujedinitelj je jugoslovenski Linkoln, kaže slavni Nikola Tesla. Protiv gnusnih laži 'austrijaka' Adamiča," *Jugoslovenska pošta*, V, 1655 (1934), 2.

849b *South Slav Herald*, November 19, 1934, p. 3.

850 Schneider, Isador. "The Macaulay Strikes: Episodes in Literary History," *Literary America*, I (October, 1934), 7-12.

851 "Topics of The Times: Our Foreign Stock," New York *Times*, November 2, 1934, p. 22.

852 Andrica, Theodore. "Andrica in Jugoslavia: Andrica Takes Time Out in Jugoslavia to Visit Relatives of Louis Adamic, Who Is Banned from Country," Cleveland *Press*, November 8, 1934, p. 1.

853 "Proletariat Readers in Libraries," "Perennial 'Wolf' Crier," and "Education for Reading," *Saturday Review of Literature*, XI (December 22, 1934), 384.

854 "Adamic and His Thirty Million," *Jewish Frontier*, II (December, 1934), 7.

855 B., Dr. "Naši Američani o Adamiču," *Pohod* (Ljubljana), III, 47 (1934), 1-2.

856 –c. "Problem Louisa Adamiča," *Borba*, II, 17 (1934), 4.

857 N., J. " 'Analiza' g. Adamiča," *Slobodna misao*, XIV, 4 (1934), 4. Cyr.

858 [Kostic, Jovan D.] "Američki pisac Luj Adamič o sebi, o Južnoj Srbiji, o Americi. . . ," *Vardar*, III, 266 (1934), 3. Cyr.

859 "Louis Adamic's 'The Native's Return,' " *Nova Doba* (Cleveland), X, 1 (1934), 3-4.

860 Lovcenski, Guslar. "Na peškoš Adamiču Luju: Zagreb," *Jugoslavenske pariske novine*, IV, 37 (1934), 1.

861 Lupis-Vukic, I[vo] F. "Akeija Louisa Adamica za iseljenike u Sjed. Državama. Kolektivne farme pod vodstvom potpornih organizacija," *Novo Doba* (Split), XVII, 87 (1934), 4.

861a *Hrvatski radiša*, XV, 4 (1934), 38-39.

862 ———. "Rad Louisa Adamiča u Americi," *Novosti* (Zagreb), XXVIII, 5 (1934), 11.

863 "Potepuh in njegovi menažerji," *Pohod* (Ljubljana), III, 44-45 (1934), 1-2.

864 "Predavanjsko potovanje Lojzeta Adamiča," *Nova Doba* (Cleveland), X, 9 (1934), 8.

865 "Slučaj g. Adamiča ili naša duhobna servilnost," *Jugoslovenska pošta*, V, 1406 (1934), 3.

866 "*The Nation*'s Honor Roll for 1934," *Nation*, CXL (January 2, 1935), 3.

867 "Adamic, Author and Lecturer Speaks at Convocation," *Connecticut College News* (New London), January 19, 1935, pp. 1, 3.

868 Rollins, William. "What Is a Proletarian Writer?" *New Masses*, XIV (January 29, 1935), 22-23.

869 Hohlfeld, Adelin. "All Around the Town," *The Capitol Times* (Madison, Wisconsin), January 30, 1935, p. 5.

870 Leben, Stanko. "Sodobna Amerika—Volta Senca," *Modra ptica*, VII (January, 1935), 40-46.

871 "The Editors," *Jewish Frontier*, II (January, 1935), 20.

872 Smith, Matthew and Samuel Romer. "Mr. Adamic's Detroit," *Nation*, CXL (March 13, 1935), 305.

873 Boynton, H. W. "Louis Adamic's New Americans: 'Grandsons' Is a Strong and Living Tale, Set in a True Sense, Peopled by Characters of Extraordinary Vitality," New York *Times*, March 24, 1935, Sec. v, p. 5.

874 Mlakar, Frank. " 'Grandsons' Is Not a Book Merely on the Immigrant, As Supposed," *Enakopravnost* (Cleveland), April 27, 1935, p. 4.

875 "Ali se zavedamo?" *Enakopravnost* (Cleveland), June 4, 1935, p. 2.

876 "Adamičev vpliv," *Enakopravnost* (Cleveland), July 31, 1935, p. 1.

877 "Amerikanische Lebensläufe," *Prager Press*, August 15, 1935, p. 6.

878 Burt, Struthers. "The Avoidance of Being American," *Scribner's Magazine*, XCVIII (August, 1935), 105-109.

879 "Australija o Adamiču," *Enakopravnost* (Cleveland), October 28, 1935, p. 2.

880 "Blackmailing of Yugoslavia," *Ujediljeno srpstvo* (Chicago), XXIX, 35, (1935), 1. Cyr.

881 McWilliams, Carey. *Louis Adamic and Shadow-America.* Los Angeles: Arthur Whipple, 1935.

882 "Najnoviji rad Louisa Adamiča i njegov veliki propagandni značaj," *Novosti* (Zagreb), XXIX, 214 (1935), 8.

883 "Napadi na Louisa Adamiča," *Slovenija* (Ljubljana), II, 45 (1935), 2.

884 "Nov roman Louisa Adamiča," *Jutro* (Ljubljana), XVI, 275 (1935), 7.

885 G., V.J. "Razgovor s pisateljem Louis Adamičem: Jutri ob 8. uri zvečer predava v Kolegiju Baldwin Wallace v Berea, Ohio," *Enakopravnost* (Cleveland), March 12, 1936, pp. 1, 4.

886 McWilliams, Carey. "Sentiment Against Aliens Held Peril to American Spirit," *Illustrated Daily News* (Los Angeles), April 13, 1936, p. 5.

887 Lupis-Vukic, I. F., "Louis Adamič, kao branilac inorodaca u Americi," *Javnost* (Beograd), May 23, 1936, pp. 478-479.

888 Denlinger, Sutherland. "The Sister of Louis Adamic Elopes into a New Novel," *New York World-Telegram*, August 19, 1936, Sec. I, p. 5.

889 H., J. "Roman jednoga 'fačuka': Novo djelo Luja Adamiča 'Zipka života,' " *Obzor*, September 12, 1936, pp. 1-2.

890 Kazin, Alfred. "A Hero with a Sense of the Historic: Mr. Adamic's Novel of Austro-Hungarian Peasants and Aristocrats before Sarajevo," New York *Times*, September 20, 1936, Sec. V, p. 5.

891 Gregory, Horace. "Stranger Than Fiction," *Nation*, CXLIII (September 26, 1936), 367.

892 [Molek, Ivan]. "Adamičeva 'Zibel življenja,' " *Prosveta*, September 30, 1936, p. 4; October 7, p. 4.

893 P[raček Krasna, Anna]. "Zibel življenja," *Prosveta*, October 9, 1936, p. 2; October 12, p. 2; October 13, p. 2; October 15, p. 2.

894 "Edward Dean Sullivan on Louis Adamic's Review," *Saturday Review of Literature*, XIV (October 10, 1936), 11.

895 "Assassination: New Light Thrown on Brutal Murder of Yugoslav Monarch," *News Review* (London), October 17, 1936.

896 "Difference of Opinion," *Nation*, CXLIII (October 31, 1936), 532.

897 Bronowicz, Józef W. "Słynny Louis Adamic w Obronie Cudzoziemców," *Ameryka-Echo* (Toledo), November 8, 1936, p. 11.

898 Lupis-Vukic, I[vo] F. "Američki pisac o L. Adamiču," *Javnost* (Beograd), II, 50 (1936), 1075-1076.

899 New York *Times* and National Association of Book Publishers. *Program: The New York Times National Book Fair*. New York: New York *Times*, 1936.

900 Trunk, J[urij] M. "Anekdota," *Amerikanski Slovenec*, XLV, 143 (1936), 2.

901 Anderson, John. "The 'Sitdown' and the I.W.W.," *Nation*, CXLIV (January 9, 1937), 55.

902 P., I. M. "Turns With a Bookworm," New York *Herald Tribune*, January 31, 1937, Sec. X, p. 14.

903 Folsom, Franklin. "Dobri princ Rudo. Kolijevka života," *Književnik* (Zagreb), X (February, 1937), 92-94.

904 "Most Useful Citizen," Cleveland *Press*, July 8, 1937, p. 12.

905 Mok, Michel. "The Ten Percenters," New York *Post*, August 12, 1937, p. 11.

906 Goldsmith, Robert. "Louis Adamic Finds His Jersey Farm Gives Him Seclusion for Writing," Easton *Express* (Pennsylvania), August 25, 1937.

907 "Studija o Louisu Adamiču," *Književnik* (Zagreb), x (August–September, 1937), 396.

908 [Grahor, Olga]. "Trideset milijonov novih Američanov," *Ljubljanski Zvon*, LVII (September–October, 1937), 482-486.

909 Lupis-Vukic, Ivo F. "Jugoslaveni u Sjedinjenim Državama. Jugoslovenski radnici—Suzalo—Adamič—Pupin—Tesla," *Iseljenički muzej* (Zagreb), III (September, 1937), 4-5.

909a *Novo doba* (Split), XX, 51 (1937), 2.

910 "Novi roman našeg poznatog pisca u U.S.A.—Louisa Adamiča," *Novi iseljenik* (Zagreb), XVI, 2 (1937), 2.

911 Lupis-Vukic, I[vo] F. "Najnovije djelo Luja Adamiča," *Javnost* (Beograd), III, 48 (1937), 909-910.

912 Hallam, Mary. "Author Seeks Complete Story of America," Pittsburgh *Sun-Telegraph*, March 14, 1938, p. 14.

913 Brooks, Obed. "Review and Comment," *New Masses*, XXVIII (July 26, 1938), 22-24.

914 Klančar, Anton J. "Cankar v angleščini," *Cankarjev Glasnik*, II (December, 1938), 127-130.

915 [Borko, Božidar]. "Nova knjiga Louisa Adamiča," *Jutro* (Ljubljana), XIX, 202 (1938), 7.

916 [Esih, Ivan]. "Nova knjiga Luja Adamiča," *Obzor*, LXXVII, 142 (1938), 2.

917 Burnham, James and Max Shachtman. "Intellectuals in Retreat: A Political Analysis of the Drift of the Anti-Stalinist Intellectuals from Marxism Towards Reform," *The New International*, V (January, 1939), 3-22.

918 [Grahor, Olga]. "Louis Adamič: Moja Amerika," *Ljubljanski Zvon*, LIX (January-February, 1939), 52-56.

919 Hickey, J. T. H. "1938's Outstanding Young Americans," *Future* (Official Publication of the U.S. Junior Chamber of Commerce), I (January, 1939), 6-7, 27-30.

920 "Louis Adamic: A Living Example of Opportunity in America," *The American Slav*, F (January, 1939), 8-9.

921 "Colonial Dame-skis," Baltimore *Evening Sun*, February 10, 1939.

922 Notice of an Adamic request for information. *Nordisk Tidende* (New York), February 16, 1939, p. 4.

923 "Ten Important Books of Non-Fiction in 1938," *Current History*, XLIX (February, 1939), 2.

924 "Book Notes," New York *Herald Tribune*, March 10, 1939, p. 19.

925 [Dabney, Virginius]. "Virginia's Racial Strains," Richmond *Times-Dispatch*, March 22, 1939, p. 8.

926 Veteran. "Americans All," Baltimore *Evening Sun*, March 28, 1939.

927 Yolles, P. P. "Naród narodów," *Nowy Swiat*, April 8, 1939.

928 "Louis Adamic Delights Us with a Visit," *Nationality Community News* (St. Paul, Minnesota), May 12, 1939, pp. 2-3.

929 Blakeman, W. Hildreth. "Answer to an Ad," Baltimore *Evening Sun*, May 13, 1939.

930 Fletcher, Frederick A. "He Disagrees with Adamic," Baltimore *Evening Sun*, May 15, 1939, p. 17.

931 Cavanaugh, Vincent D. "Anglo-Saxons and Their So-Called Flair for Freedom," Baltimore *Evening Sun*, May 16, 1939, p. 21.

932 Speier, Ursula. "Broadmindedness of the Founders," Baltimore *Evening Sun*, May 18, 1939.

933 Andrews, Matthew Page. "More about Immigrants, Anglo-Saxons, American Institutions, and So Forth," Baltimore *Evening Sun*, May 19, 1939.

934 Morrow, W. Don. "Says Our Government Is Anglo-Saxon," Baltimore *Evening Sun*, May 24, 1939.

935 Brown, Nils F:son. "En nation av nationer," *California Veckoblad*, July 13, 1939, p. 4.

936 [Curčin, Milan], and Aleksije Jelačič. "Siluete savremene Amerike," *Nova Evropa*, XXXII (September, 1939), 308-310.

937 Bonanno, Raoul Spoleti. "Louis Adamic Asks Questions," *L'Araldo* (Cleveland), December 15, 1939, p. 11.

938 [Jacobs, Sidney J.]. "A Nation of Nations," *The Advocate: A Weekly Journal of Jewish News and Views*, LXCVIII (December 22, 1939), 1.

939 [Katic, Milan]. " 'The Woman from Croatia': Interesantna novela Louisa Adamiča štampana u velikoj philadelphijskoj reviji, mk," *Novosti* (Zagreb), XXXIII, 309 (1939), 13.

940 L-V., I. F. "Louis Adamič o Jugoslaviji i Jugoslavenima," *Nova riječ*, IV, 157 (1939), 9.

941 ———. "Sjedinjene države: Nacija naroda. Jedan smjeli i veliki pothvat našega Louisa Adamiča," *Novo dobo* (Split), XXII, 84 (1939), 17-18.

942 [Christopher, Louis C.]. "We Meet Louis Adamic: A Yugoslav Selected as One of the 'Ten Outstanding Young Americans,' " *American-Yugoslav Reflector*, I (January, 1940), 11-13.

943 "Mr. Dies Goes to Town," *Propaganda Analysis*, III (January, 1940), 1-10.

944 "Vanka's Art Brings Fame to Church," *American-Yugoslav Reflector*, I (January, 1940), 14-15.

945 Lupis-Vukic, I. F. "O Louisa Adamiču," *Vidici* (Beograd), March 25, 1940, pp. 169-170.

946 "Interview Louisa Adamiča," *Prosveta*, August 1, 1940, p. 3.

946a *Glas naroda*, August 6, 1940, p. 3.

947 "Melting Pot or Mosaic?" *The B'nai B'rith Messenger*, August 9, 1940, p. 4.

948 Hansen, Harry. "The First Reader," New York *World-Telegram*, September 12, 1940, p. 23.

949 Andrica, Theodore. "American Unity Council Holds First Meeting," Cleveland *Press*, November 9, 1940.

950 "Bil je lep večer," *Enakopravnost* (Cleveland), November 23, 1940, p. 2.

951 "Unity Council Makes Its Bow," *Enakopravnost* (Cleveland), November 23, 1940, p. 4.

952 Krajger, Vito. "Delo Luis-ja Adamiča v Združenih Državah Sev. Amerike," *Obzorja*, III (November, 1940), 441-446.

953 ———. "Revija: 'Common Ground' . . . Vito Krajger," *Ljubljanski Zvon*, LX (November–December, 1940), 619-621.

954 "Authors at Christmas," *Saturday Review of Literature*, XXIII (December 28, 1940), 11.

955 VanGelder, Robert. "Louis Adamic on His New Series of Books," New York *Times*, December 29, 1940, Sec. VI, p. 2.

955a *Writers and Writing* (New York, 1946), pp. 152-155.

956 Committee of the American Common. Mimeograph of "Wall of Fame of the American Common, World's Fair of 1940 in New York." New York: Committee of the American Common, [1940].

957 K[atic], M[ilan]. "Louis Adamič stvara novu Ameriku. Iz 50 različitih narodnosti postaje nova američka nacija. Veliki pokret književnika naše kriv," *Novosti* (Zagreb), XXXIV, 91 (1940), 13.

958 Lupis-Vukic, I[vo] F. " 'Common Ground' pod uredništvom Louisa Adamiča. Organ zajedničkog vijeca za američko jedinstvo," *Novosti* (Zagreb), XXXIV, 355 (1940), prilog, 41-42.

959 ———. "Nova Adamičeva pripovijetka: 'Stari inozemac pri kuhinjskom prozoru.' Adamičeva inicijativa: 'Zajedničko vijece za američko jedinstvo.' Jugoslaven na najvišem državnom položaju u Americi. Književnik Adamič član 'Savjetodavne komisije Vijeca za narodnu obranu U.S.A.,' " *Novosti* (Zagreb), XXXIV, 197 (1940), 13.

960 ———. "Novo djelo Louisa Adamiča 'Iz mnogih zemalja,' koje je napisao nakon bezbrojnih .... starog slovenskog useljenika seljaka," *Novosti* (Zagreb), XXXIV, 329 (1940), 17.

961 ———. " 'Zajedničar' o Louisa Adamiču i njegovoj 'zena iz Hrvatske,' " *Nova riječ*, V, 167 (1940), 8.

962 "Nova Adamičeva knjiga," *Slovenija* (Ljubljana), IX, 48 (1940), 4.

963 [Senoa, Vera]. "Luis Adamič und sein 'Land aller Länder': Wie ein slowenischer Bauernjunge ein weltbekannter Schriftsteller wurde," *Morgenblatt*, LV, 12 (1940), 9-10.

964 "Slovan a pritel Cechu," *Amerikán Národni Kalendár (Svornost)* (Chicago, 1940), p. 101.

965 "Author, Author!" *Saturday Review of Literature*, XXIII (February 8, 1941), 22.

966 "Gets Prize for Best Book of '40 on Racial Relations," New York *Times*, February 13, 1941, p. 16.

967 "Anisfield Award," *Saturday Review of Literature*, XXIII (February 15, 1941), 8.

968 Photograph of Adamic as recipient of honorary degree, Temple University. Philadelphia *Inquirer*, February 15, 1941, p. 12.

969 "Turn Fifth Column on Nazis, U.S. Urged," New York *Times*, April 4, 1941, p. 18.

970 " 'American Unity' Dinner," *Common Ground*, I (Summer, 1941), 111-114.

971 Stolberg, Benjamin. "The Un-Americanizers," *American Mercury*, LIII (September, 1941), 360-366.

972 Mann, Klaus. "Profile of the Month: Louis Adamic," *Decision*, II (October, 1941), 76-79.

973 Abingdon, A. "Black Lamb and Grey Falcon," *Saturday Review of Literature*, XXIV (November 1, 1941), 11.

974 "Women Scholars Active in Wartime: Throughout World They Work for Post-War Cooperation, University Group Hears," New York *Times*, November 9, 1941, p. 24.

975 Lyons, Leonard. "The Lyons Den," New York *Post*, November 15, 1941, p. 9.

976 "Hoover Food Plan Scored," New York *Times*, November 16, 1941, p. 21.

977 Ambrožič, O. F. M. Bernard. "Jeremija se skuša rešiti. Beseda o Lojzu Adamiču," *Glas naroda*, November 26, 1941, p. 4.

978 J[ontez], I[van]. "Adamič ima načrt za mir," *Cankarjev glasnik*, V (November, 1941), 57-59.

979 Becker, May L. " 'Twenty Books Across Sea' To Be Exhibited Here Tuesday," New York *Herald Tribune*, December 4, 1941, p. 24.

980 "Citizens' Group Formed to Help U.S. Win War," New York *Herald Tribune*, December 21, 1941, p. 18.

981 Kostrzewski, M. J. "Two-Way Passage," *The Medical and Dental Bulletin* (Official Organ of the Polish Medical and Dental Association of America), XIII (December, 1941), 132-133.

982 Fink, Joseph L. *Two-Way Passage: A Radio Address.* Buffalo: WBEN, 1941.

983 Kavaja, Marko. "U grupi posleratnih američkih književnika i otkrovitelja Nove Amerike ističe se i jedan Jugosloven," *Vreme*, XXI, 6889 (1941), 14. Cyr.

984 Roosevelt, Eleanor. "My Day" columns for December 18, 1941, and January 16, 1942, in any of Mrs. Roosevelt's many places of syndication.

985 "Story of Gary to Be Told on Screen by Louis Adamic," Gary *Post-Tribune* (Indiana), February 17, 1942, p. 2.

986 "Sidelines," *This Week Magazine*, August 23, 1942, p. 2.

987 J[ontez], I[van]. "Književnost," *Cankarjev glasnik*, VI (September, 1942), 53-54.

988 Trivanovitch, Vaso. "After Victory—What?" *Yugoslavia*, I (November 14, 1942), 4.

989 "The Louis Adamics Live Here," *House and Garden*, LXXXII (November, 1942), 44-45.

990 [Alpert, Carl]. "The Adamic Plan," *New Palestine*, XXXIII (December 4, 1942), 4-5.

991 Trivanovitch, Vaso. "Inside Yugoslavia," *Yugoslavia*, I (December 15, 1942), 1, 8; II (January 6, 1943), 1-2.

992 "Marco Polo Adamic," *Saturday Evening Post*, CCXV (December 19, 1942), 4.

993 Rice, John Andrew. *I Came Out of the Eighteenth Century* (New York, 1942), pp. 328-341.

994 Grafton, Samuel. "This Is All One World," *Yugoslavia*, II (January 6, 1943), 11-12.

995 Sternberger, Estelle M. "If Revolution Should Sweep Europe," *Yugoslavia*, II (January 6, 1943), 9-10.

996 Swing, Raymond Grand. "This Is Not Yugoslavia Alone," *Yugoslavia*, II (January 6, 1943), 10.

997 "The Caves of Europe," *Time Magazine*, January 11, 1943, pp. 31-32.

998 Bukovinski, Ivan. "Sobotne misli," *Glas naroda*, February 1, 1943, p. 4.

999 "Quotations from the 'Srbobran,' " *Slobodna Reč* (Pittsburgh), February 18, 1943, p. 4.

1000 "LaGuardia Is Set for Army Service in Brigadier Rank: Albert Spalding, Louis Adamic and Ugo Carusi Reported To Be His North African Aides," New York *Times*, March 28, 1943, pp. 1, 12.

1001 "Louis Adamič bo nastopil mesto pri La Guardiovi misiji v Afriki," *Glas naroda*, March 31, 1943, p. 1.

1002 Steel, Johannes. "Steel Filings: Call for a Volunteer State Department," New York *Post*, April 10, 1943, p. 21.

1002a *Yugoslavia*, II (April 26, 1943), 3.

1003 Markovic, Mirko. "Još jedna sramota," *Slobodna Reč* (Pittsburgh), April 27, 1943, p. 2. Cyr.

1004 "Zašto fašisti urlaju na Luisa Adamiča," *Slobodna Reč* (Pittsburgh), July 7, 1943, p. 2. Cyr.

1005 Adamič sazvao sednicu Ujedinjenog odbora Južnih Slovena u Klivlend 7 avgusta," *Slobodna Reč* (Pittsburgh), August 4, 1943, p. 1. Cyr.

1005a "Adamic Calls Yugoslav Meeting: Hits Activities of Yugoslav Government in Exile," *Slobodna Reč* (Pittsburgh), August 6, 1943, p. 4.

1006 "S. S. Nikola Tesla," *The Bulletin of the United Committee of South-Slavic Americans*, I (October 1, 1943), 8.

1007 "My Native Land," *Slobodna Reč* (Pittsburgh), October 6, 1943, p. 3. Cyr.

1007a *Slobodna Reč*, November 22, 1943, p. 4.

1008 "Tesla and the Future," *The Bulletin of the United Committee of South-Slavic Americans*, I (October 20, 1943), 5.

1009 "Kosanovic, Adamič i Balokovic dolaze u Okland, Kalifornija," *Slobodna Reč* (Pittsburgh), October 22, 1943, p. 3. Cyr.

1010 "My Native Land," *Yugoslavia*, II (November 3, 1943), 10.

1011 "Announcement," *The Argonaut*, November 12, 1943, p. 19.

1012 " 'Njujork Tajms' o novoj knjizi Lujza Adamiča," *Slobodna Reč* (Pittsburgh), November 15, 1943, p. 3. Cyr.

1013 [Praček Krasna, Anna]. "Moja rodna dežela," *Glas naroda*, November 24, 1943, p. 2; November 26, p. 2.

1014 Remnyi, Joseph. "Louis Adamic: A Portrait," *College English*, v (November, 1943), 62-70.

1015 "Fight on Fascism Urged by Adamic," New York *Times*, December 13, 1943, p. 7.

1016 "Ameriška armada izdala Adamičevo knjigo za ameriške vojake," *Glas naroda*, December 17, 1943, p. 2.

1017 "American Serbs Greet People's Government in Jugoslavia," *Slobodna Reč* (Pittsburgh), December 20, 1943, p. 4.

1018 "Slavs or Americans?" Pittsburgh *Press*, December 22, 1943, p. 18.

1019 "Browder Appeals to Liberal Forces: Urges Unity on Basis of Policy Laid Down by Dimitroff of Reichstag Fire Fame," New York *Times*, December 23, 1943, p. 4.

1020 Maletic, S[trahinja]. " 'Slobodna Jugoslavija' pozdravlja Luisa Adamiča i B. Furlana," *Slobodna Reč* (Pittsburgh), December 27, 1943, p. 3. Cyr.

1021 Cook, Eric. "Značenje nove vijesti o Jugoslaviji. Izjava Adamiča i izbjeglog partizana," *Napredak* (Sidney), N.S. I, 18 (1943), 1.

1022 "Dolazak Adamiča u Toronto," *Srpski glasnik*, III, 46 (1943), 2. Cyr.

1023 "Jugoslovanski izseljenici v Amerik so obsodili izdajstvo Bele Garde in Mihajlovicevcev ter z občudovanjem priznali edino pravilno pot osvobodilne fronte in narodno-osvobodilne vojske Jugoslavije (Pittsburška resolucija)," *Ljudska pravica*, VII, 8 (1943), 7.

1024 K. "Louis Adamič: 'Moja rodna gruda,'" *Novosti* (Toronto), III, 402 (1943), 4.

1025 Union of Slovenian Parishes of America. *Shall Slovenia Be Sovietized? A Rebuttal to Louis Adamic, Gathered and Translated from the Pages of the Slovenian Daily "Ameriška domovina."* Cleveland, 1943.

1026 Zelle, Joe. "Louis Adamic," *Slovenski koledar*, Vol. XXX (1943), pp. 213-216.

1027 Mikalački, K. "Sa Slovenskog zbora u Milvoki," *Slobodna Reč* (Pittsburgh), January 14, 1944, p. 3. Cyr.

1028 Dennen, Leon. "The Riddle of Yugoslavia," *American Mercury*, LVIII (February, 1944), 194-202.

1029 "Louis Adamič za polno priznanje Tita," *Glas naroda*, March 8, 1944, p. 1.

1030 Murnich, Joseph. "Pisatelj Louis Adamič," *Glas naroda*, March 10, 1944, p. 3.

1031 *Congressional Record: Proceedings and Debates of the 78th Congress*, Second Session, Vol. XC, pt. 2 (Washington, D. C., 1944), pp. 2548-2550. Remarks of Fred E. Busbey, March 13, 1944.

1032 Demir, Hasim. "Naši muslimani za jedinstvo u borbi protiv fašizma. Cikago, Illinois," *Slobodna Reč* (Pittsburgh), March 13, 1944, p. 3. Cyr.

1033 Markovic, Mirko. "Pravo govora u Geri," *Slobodna Reč* (Pittsburgh), March 13, 1944, p. 2. Cyr.

1034 "Hoffman Charges Reds Set Policies," New York *Times*, March 14, 1944, p. 36.

1035 Maravic, Duro. "Još nekoliko reči o Adamičevoj skupštini u Geri," *Slobodna Reč* (Pittsburgh), March 29, 1944, p. 3. Cyr.

1036 "Potrebno je zaustaviti neprijateljsku propagandu Srbobrana," *Slobodna Reč* (Pittsburgh), March 29, 1944, p. 2. Cyr.

1037 "Važna obavest ujedinj. odbora Južnoslovenskih Amerikanaca," *Slobodna Reč* (Pittsburgh), May 1, 1944, p. 3. Cyr.

1038 "Važna vest iz Združenega odbora južnoslovanskih Amerikancev," *Glas naroda*, May 3, 1944, p. 2.

1039 Notice of Adamic's withdrawal as President of the United Committee of South-Slavic Americans. *The Bulletin of the United Committee of South-Slavic Americans*, II (May 10, 1944), 3.

1040 Drenovac, Nikola. "Nije to brevijar nego borba," *Slobodna Reč* (Pittsburgh), June 13, 1944, p. 3. Cyr.

1041 "Fotitch Dismissal Step for Tito Accord: Ambassador's Rift with Adamic Group a Factor," New York *Times*, June 13, 1944, p. 7.

1042 "Artists Back Roosevelt," *Slobodna Reč* (Pittsburgh), August 8, 1944, p. 4.

1043 "Maršal Tito piše Louisu Adamiču," *Slobodna Reč* (Pittsburgh), September 12, 1944, p. 1. Cyr.

1044 "Titova poruka," *Slobodna Reč* (Pittsburgh), September 12, 1944, p. 2. Cyr.

1045 Tito, J. B. "Tito's Letter to Louis Adamic," *The Bulletin of the United Committee of South-Slavic Americans*, II (September 15, 1944), 4-5.

1046 "Louis Adamic To Be Honored," New York *Times*, September 20, 1944, p. 14.

1047 Tito, J. B. "Dragocena je pomoc Jugoslovena iz Amerike," *Slobodna Reč* (Pittsburgh), September 23, 1944, p. 2. Cyr.

1047a "Tito's Fine Letter to Louis Adamic," *Slobodna Reč*, October 10, 1944, p. 4.

1048 Popovič, Stevan. "Sa pesmom u borbu," *Slobodna Reč* (Pittsburgh), October 3, 1944, p. 3, Cyr.

1049 "Adamic Appeals for War Fund," *Slobodna Reč* (Pittsburgh), November 8, 1944, p. 4.

1050 Sandburg, Carl. "Carl Sandburg," Chicago *Sunday Times*, December 31, 1944, p. 7.

1051 "Luji Adamič i srpski fašisti," *Srpski glasnik*, IV, 3 (1944), 3, 4. Cyr.

1052 "Obaveštenje Odbora Juž. Slovena Amerike," *Srpski glasnik*, IV, 18 (1944), 2, 4. Cyr.

1053 "Pismo maršala Tita Louisu Adamiču, New York," *Novosti* (Toronto), IV, 561 (1944), 3.

1054 "Americans from Yugoslavia," *The Bulletin of the United Committee of South-Slavic Americans*, III (January–February, 1945), 9.

1055 "Letter from England," "Letter from a Soldier," and " 'My Native Land' Translated," *The Bulletin of the United Committee of South-Slavic Americans*, III (January–February, 1945), 10, 11, 16.

1056 "Ilustrirana knjiga o borbi naroda v Jugoslaviji, *Glas naroda*, March 27, 1945, p. 2.

1057 Bentley, Eric R. "Report from the Academy," *Partisan Review*, XII (Summer, 1945), 422-430.

1058 "Child Book Award Presented for '45 . . . Adamic Assails Our History Texts," New York *Times*, November 13, 1945, p. 18.

1059 Nevins, Allan. "Allen Nevins Praises Louis Adamic for His Spirited Defense of Our Racial Minorities: Takes Exception to the Idea of 'Hyphenated Americans,' " New York *Post*, December 6, 1945, p. 3.

1060 Zyskind, Harold. "Louis Adamic and His Work," *Chicago Jewish Forum*, V (Winter, 1946), 129-134.

1061 *Congressional Record: Proceedings and Debates of the 79th Congress*, Second Session, Vol. XCII, pt. 3 (Washing, D. C., 1946), pp. 2958-2959. Remarks of John E. Rankin, April 2, 1946.

1062 Akers, Milburn P. "Liberals Adopt Program with Political Objectives," Chicago *Sun*, September 29, 1946, pp. 1, 3.

1063 "Early Comments on 'Dinner at the White House' " and "Louis Adamic's New Book 'Dinner at the White House,' " *The Bulletin of the United Committee of South-Slavic Americans*, IV (September, 1946), 30, 31.

1064 "Churchill Sues Adamic and Publisher for Libel," New York *Times*, October 25, 1946, p. 5.

1065 Matchan, Don C. "Roosevelt and Churchill, and the Peace," *The Bulletin of the United Committee of South-Slavic Americans*, IV (December, 1946), 31-32.

1066 Avery, Andrew. *The Communist Fifth Column*. Chicago, 1946. "Noted Writers, Actors, Artists and Professors Follow Party Line, Espouse Red Causes," pp. 27-29.

1067 Hampton, Vernon B. *Threat to American Unity: A Reply to Mr. Adamic*. Staten Island, [ca. 1946].

1068 "Churchill Wins 'Substantial' Libel Damages in Out-of-Court Settlement on Adamic Book," New York *Times*, January 16, 1947, p. 23.

1069 "Miscellany," *Newsweek*, January 20, 1947, p. 18.

1070 "Footnote to Libel," *Newsweek*, January 27, 1947, p. 32.

1071 Blinov, E. "From the History of Anglo-American Relations," *New Times*, April 18, 1947, pp. 25-27.

1072 "Monopolists Plot Hate Drive Against USSR, Adamic Asserts," Valley City *Times-Record* (North Dakota), May 16, 1947, p. 2.

1073 Rubin, V. "Dinner at the White House," *Bolshevik*, XXIV (June 30, 1947), 58-64. Cyr.

1074 "Louis Adamic Says Story of His Speech Was Misconstrued," *Delaware Valley News* (Frenchtown, New Jersey), December 12, 1947, pp. 1, 4.

1075 "Appeal to Voters in Italy Assailed: Protest Wire Sent to Truman by Group Here Opposed to Anti-Communist Drive," New York *Times*, April 15, 1948, p. 8.

1076 "Rev. Begany Defends Catholicism's Allegiance in Answer to Adamic," *Cement News* (Northampton, Pennsylvania), June 10, 1948, pp. 1, 13.

1077 DaCosta, Sidney A. "Louis Adamic's Viewpoint on Yugoslavian-Cominform Rift," *Delaware Valley News* (Frenchtown, New Jersey), July 16, 1948, pp. 1, 2.

1078 Kilgallen, James L. "Wallace Named: Urges U.S. Give Berlin to Reds," New York *Journal American*, July 25, 1948, pp. 1, 2.

1079 "Red Woman Spy Lists Currie and White, Top FDR Aides, As Sources for War Secrets: Insists Many Others in Hush-Hush Jobs Gave Data for Russia," Philadelphia *Inquirer*, August 1, 1948, pp. 1, 4.

1080 "Red 'Fifth Column' Mines Givernment, Budenz Testifies," New York *Times*, August 3, 1948, pp. 1, 10.

1081 "Ex-Communist Heard; Accused Charge Smear," New York *Star*, August 4, 1948, pp. 1, 4.

1082 "Two Hiss Brothers Deny Red Charges . . . Adamic Sees Wallace Smear Attempt," New York *Times*, August 4, 1948, p. 3.

1083 Heath, S. Burton. "Wallace Backers," Tiffin *Advertiser-Tribune* (Ohio), August 10, 1948. This syndicated article, often with a more menacing title, appeared in many such newspapers on or about this date; for example, in the Austin *Statesman* (Texas), the Sandusky *Register-Star-News* (Ohio), the Fort Collins *Coloradoan*, and the Falls City *Journal* (Nebraska).

1084 "A Reader Questions Adamic's Rebuttal," *Delaware Valley News* (Frenchtown, New Jersey), August 13, 1948, p. 3.

1085 Kinnaird, Clark, "Kinnaird, Adamic Continue Debate," *Delaware Valley News* (Frenchtown, New Jersey), August 27, 1948.

1068 "Letter Box: Anti-Adamic; Anti-Kinnaird," *Delaware Valley News* (Frenchtown, New Jersey), September 3, 1948, p. 2.

1087 Teague, Walter D. "Teague Picks Up Where Kinnaird Left Off in Adamic Controversy," *Delaware Valley News* (Frenchtown, New Jersey), September 17, 1948, p. 3.

1088 Lea, Victor L. "Economist Lea Challenges Adamic to 'Town Hall' Debate Here," *Delaware Valley News* (Frenchtown, New Jersey), September 24, 1948, p. 3.

1089 Walsh, Mike. "Bucks County Irishman Enters Kinnaird-Adamic-Teague Debate," *Delaware Valley News* (Frenchtown, New Jersey), September 24, 1948, p. 3.

1090 Fleming, Walter N. "Columnist Sounds Taps," *Delaware Valley News*, (Frenchtown, New Jersey), October 1, 1948, p. 2.

1091 Kinnaird, Clark. "Kinnaird Rejoins," *Delaware Valley News* (Frenchtown, New Jersey), October 1, 1948, pp. 2-3.

1092 "Adamic to Talk Friday," *Bandwagon (Nisei for Wallace)*, I (October 26, 1948), 1, 6.

1093 "U.S. Slav Congress Called Soviet Tool," New York *Times*, June 26, 1949, pp. 1, 34.

1094 Committee on Un-American Activities, House of Representatives. *Report on the American Slav Congress and Associated Organizations*. Washington, D. C., June 26, 1949.

1095 Pucova, Mira. "Louis Adamič in Amerika," *Novi Svet* (Ljubljana), IV (1949), 381-389.

1096 "New Peace Policy Urged on Truman: 159 Citizens in Letter Ask for Halting of the Economic Conflict and Arms Race," New York *Times*, February 6, 1950, p. 5.

1097 "Foundations Face Inquiry by House," New York *Times*, August 2, 1951, p. 13.

1098 "Louis Adamic a Suicide; Found Shot, Home Afire," New York *World-Telegram and Sun*, September 4, 1951, pp. 1, 2.

1099 "Louis Adamic Found Dead in Farmhouse near Riegelsville with Rifle on Knees," Easton *Express* (Pennsylvania), September 4, 1951, pp. 1, 14.

1100 "Louis Adamic Shot Dead in Burning Home," New York *Journal American*, September 4, 1951, p. 1.

1101 "Author Adamic Is Found Dead in Burning House," Milwaukee *Sentinel*, September 5, 1951, p. 7.

1102 "Author Louis Adamic Dies of Bullet Wound," Los Angeles *Times*, September 5, 1951, pt. 1, p. 19.

1103 "Find Adamic Shot to Death in Fiery Home," Chicago *Tribune*, September 5, 1951, pp. 1, 6.

1104 "Shot, Adamic Dies in Burning House," Chicago *Daily Sun-Times*, September 5, 1951.

1105 "Adamic Slain, Friend's View: Threats Are Related" and "Suicide, Widow Thinks," Milwaukee *Journal*, September 7, 1951, p. 6.

1106 Beckett, Henry. "Adamic Buried in N.J. Without Rites," New York *Post*, September 7, 1951, p. 54.

1107 Berger, Meyer. "Adamic Dies of Shot, Home Aflame; Final Verdict Studied in Jersey," *Prosveta*, September 12. 1951, p. 1.

1108 Blum, R. "Louis Adamic," *Review of International Affairs*, II (September 12, 1951), 11.

1109 Brinocar, Mary. "Tribute to Louis Adamic," *Prosveta*, September 12, 1951, p. 1.

1110 Lotrich, Donald J. "Flashes," *Prosveta*, September 12, 1951, p. 1.

1111 "Mystery Killing," *Time Magazine*, September 17, 1951, p. 26.

1112 Aronson, James. "Louis Adamic—American," *National Guardian*, September 19, 1951, p. 12.

1113 McWilliams, Carey. "Louis Adamic, American," *Nation*, CLXXIII (September 22, 1951), 230-232.

113a *Prosveta*, September 26, 1951, pp. 1, 8.

1114 Ironick, I. " 'Mourn Not the Dead,' " *Prosveta*, September 26, 1951, p. 1.

1115 P., F. "Louis Adamic," *Prosveta*, September 26, 1951, p. 2.

1116 Beckett, Henry. "Adamic's Neighbors Can't Believe Author Could Have Killed Himself," New York *Post*, September 30, 1951, pp. 5, 21.

1117 Bubnic, Albin. "Pomenek z bratom," *Primorski Dnevnik*, September 30, 1951, p. 3.

1118 "Usoda Trsta mu je bila vedno pri srcu," *Primorski Dnevnik*, September 30, 1951, p. 3.

1119 Szulc, Tad. "Adamic Death Believed Murder," *Prosveta*, October 17, 1951, p. 2.

1120 Schurmacher, Emile C. "Stalin Can Kill You," *Stag*, III (May 1952), 20-21, 66.

1121 G[radišnik], J[anez]. "Louis Adamič," *Naša žena* (Ljubljana), XI, 1 (1952), 11-12.

1122 Kristan, Cvetko A. "Louis Adamič med drugo svetovno vojno za staro domovino," *Tovariš* (Ljubljana), VIII, 52 (1952), 1111-1112.

1123 Rogelj, Janko N. "Louis Adamič kronist in slikar naših izseljencev, njihov in naš genij," *Primorski Dnevnik*, VIII, 120 (1952), 2116.

1124 Kuhel, Mirko G. "Louis Adamič—veliki človek, veliki Slovenec," *Slovenski izseljenski koledar* (Ljubljana, 1954), pp. 80-87.

1125 K[ristan], Cv[etko] A. "Kaj obsega Adamičeva književna zapuščina?" *Naši razgledi* (Ljubljana), III, 31 (1954), 7.

1126 "Literarna zapuščina Louisa Adamič," *Tovariš* (Ljubljana), X, 27 (1954), 576.

1127 S[molinsky], M[ile]. "V Grosupljem so odkrili spominsko ploščo Louisu Adamiču," *Slovenski poročevalec* (Ljubljana), XV, 191 (1954).

1128 Hofman, Branko. "Američan slovenskega rodu," *Večer*, XII, 193 (1956).

1129 "$12,350 Is Dug Out of Author's Home," New York *Times*, August 2, 1957, p. 10.

1130 Seliškar, Tone. "Louis Adamič (1899–1951)," *Slovenski izseljenski koledar* (Ljubljana, 1957), pp. 58-63.

1131 Christian, Henry A. "Fitzgerald and 'Superman': An Unpublished Letter to Louis Adamic," *Fitzgerald Newsletter*, No. 31 (Fall, 1965), 1-3.

1132 ———. "Ten Letters to Louis Adamic," *The Princeton University Library Chronicle*, XXVIII (Winter, 1967), 76-94.

1133 ———. "Louis Adamic: Immigrant and American Liberal," unpublished dissertation, Brown University, 1967.

1134 Neidle, Cecyle S. *The New Americans* (New York, 1967), pp. 279-283.

1135 Gottesmann, Ronald. "Louis Adamic and Upton Sinclair: The Record of a Friendship," *Acta Neophilologica* (Ljubljana), I (1968), 41-65.

1136 Adamič, France. "Spominski muzej Louisa Adamiča," *Zbornik Občine Grosuplje: Gospodarska, Kulturna in Zgodovinska Kronika* (Grosuplje), I (1969), 175-177.

1137 Dedijer, Vladimir. "Skrivnostina smrt Louisa Adamiča." *Izgubljeni boj J. V. Stalin: 1948-1953*, pp. 263-279. Ljubljana: C. G. P. Delo, 1969.

1137a "The Mysterious Death of Louis Adamic." *The Battle Stalin Lost: Memoirs of Yugoslavia 1948-1953*, pp. 234-248. New York: Viking, 1971.

1138 Kurent, Tine. "Valvazorjeve Praproče in nijihove poznejše prezidave," *Zbornik Občine Grosuplje: Gospodarska, Kulturna in Zgodovinska Kronika* (Grosuplje), I (1969), 167-173.

1139 Halper, Albert. "The Bookish Establishment" and "The Long, Long Journey of Louis Adamic." *Good-bye, Union Square: A Writer's Memoir of the Thirties*, pp. 139-143 and 192-202 resp. Chicago: Quadrangle Books, 1970.

Index of Authors and Editors